Aussie Rules Football

An Outsider's Perspective

Don Warner

AUSSIE RULES FOOTBALL - An Outsider's Perspective

For information visit:

donaldwarner.com

ISBN-978-0-6450315-0-8

Book and Cover design by Don Warner

Cover Photo: VFL Park Carlton vs Collingwood 30/4/1988

Book Formatting by Richard Elliot Barnes

This book is for all those who follow the great game of Australian Rules Football.

About this book

This book was inspired during the prolonged Covid-19 lockdown in Melbourne in 2020. Since there were no AFL footy games between 22nd March - 11th June I got an idea to start doing some in-depth study into Australia's most popular football code, Australian Rules football. Each week I wrote an article based on research I was doing (mainly on *Wikipedia*) and shared these articles with about 100 friends who participate in footy tipping competitions with me. Providing some interesting reading material proved to be a great way to keep in touch with people during the many months when we were not allowed to see our friends in person or travel more than 5 km from home. I felt it was worth preserving the articles, which include some personal recollections of the game we love, in book format for others to enjoy. The long-time footy followers will enjoy 'revisiting' some of your team's best moments; for new and recent followers of the sport this book will provide a useful background to how our great game evolved in Victoria from the late 1800s through to today, including stories on all 18 AFL teams.

Topics covered in the book

The book starts with a snapshot of the unusual 2020 AFL season including some interesting information about this low-scoring year, the locations and frequency of matches and a brief summary of the 2020 finals. Subsequent chapters mainly relate to ***selected aspects*** of the histories of the 18 AFL teams, team rivalries, great indigenous players, great coaches and great goal kickers. A lot of statistics are quoted and there are even some fun trivia questions to test the knowledgeable footy followers. Most chapters have a strong historical slant - the team histories are an overview rather than an in-depth analysis. 'Teams of the Century' are included in this second edition.

I have tried to connect everything by providing a further overview on the evolution of the game in Victoria from 1858, including the 1896 VFA/VFL split and the development of the 2 leagues during the 20th century. I provide an explanation on how the various Finals' systems work(ed), touch on State of Origin and recall times when football was once played almost exclusively on Saturday afternoons. Near the end of the book, I take a look at the modern era including recruiting, transfers, the draft, salary cap and the league's equalisation efforts.

Cross Referencing: There is a considerable amount of cross-referencing in the book. For example, stories about the various team rivalries appear in the team histories of *both* teams; the great goal kickers, indigenous players and coaches written about collectively in the relevant chapters are also included under the relevant team history pages on an individual basis.

Don Warner December 2020

What Readers Are Saying...

Through the strangest of football seasons due to Covid-19, I really enjoyed reading the articles and learning and revisiting football memories made familiar from a near lifetime of living in Melbourne. Rather like meeting an old friend, each article was a pleasure to read. **Andrew Mulholland**

We all love the weekly and sometimes daily drama football provides us with. What is forgotten in the ongoing AFL soap opera is the history of the game, the story behind the club we love and the clubs we hate, the background to club rivalries, who were the great players and goal kickers and how the AFL came to be what it is. Don Warner's book fills the footy history gap. Don brings an outsider's curiosity to his task and uncovers a history rich with political machination and larger than life characters. We highly recommend Don's fascinating book which will help inform those daily footy dramas. **John Coldham & Melinda Kemp**

Don is the only person I know who could turn the weekly footy tipping email folder into a historical review of the AFL. As a foreign entrant (but one of Australia's newest citizens), I am pleased to admit that most of what I now know about the AFL's history comes from a fellow North American. **Cindy**

Bors

It was exciting to read the history of the Footy (AFL) through Don's articles every week. His knowledge on the subject combined with his style of writing made it a very interesting and informative read. ***Lakshmi Saripalli***

Don has retraced the intricate history of football in a delightful book which brings so many memories of the great game to life. ***Sean Hogan***

About the Author

Don Warner was born in Toronto Canada and migrated to Australia at age 25. He grew up enjoying the sports of ice hockey, gridiron and baseball. Don settled in Melbourne in 1985 and now follows all of Australia's major sports. He has developed a keen interest in Australian Rules football over many years and supports Carlton in the AFL. Don is a former history teacher and office manager who has enjoyed writing for many years. He compiled/edited a bi-monthly office newsletter for a large professional services firm for 18 years and has written four biographies for friends.

Don is also the self-published author of two books.

Nanton Avenue Photobook - 1950s to 1970s (2016)

Beyond the Tip - Tales of the Icebergers of Brighton (2019)

Acknowledgements

Richard Barnes - for his invaluable assistance and advice in how to create an ebook for all mobile devices and for his wise advice on production matters.

Carolyn Warner - for her proof-reading assistance and keen eye for detail.

Warren Fisher and the team at Snap Printing, Notting Hill

CONTENTS

Important Dates

1858 First game played between Scotch College & Melbourne Grammar. Melbourne FC is formed.

1877 VFA is formed.

1896 VFL is formed when 8 clubs from the VFA vote to break away from the VFA to form a new league. Melbourne, South Melbourne, Geelong, Essendon, Fitzroy, and Collingwood are the main instigators of the split and invite Carlton & St Kilda to join them.

1897 First season of play in the VFL.

1908 VFL expands to 10 teams when Richmond join from the VFA and a new club called University join.

1914-18 During World War I, the short-lived University team fold at the end of 1914 after only 7 seasons and in 1916 due to wartime restrictions, the league is temporarily reduced to only 4 teams (Carlton, Collingwood, Fitzroy, Richmond).

1925 VFL expands to 12 teams, welcoming Footscray, Hawthorn and North Melbourne from the VFA.

1942-43 During World War II, the league is briefly reduced to 11 teams when Geelong is forced to withdraw its team due to wartime travel restrictions.

1982 The financially-struggling club South Melbourne play all their home matches in Sydney before officially becoming the Sydney Swans from the 1983 season. Their move to Sydney marks the start of the VFL's national expansion.

1987 VFL expands to 14 teams when the Brisbane Bears and West Coast Eagles join the league.

1990 VFL rebrands itself as the AFL to reflect the move towards a truly national competition.

1991 Adelaide Crows join.

1995 Fremantle Dockers join.

1996 Brisbane Lions is formed after a merger between Fitzroy Lions & Brisbane Bears. Footscray FC rebrand themselves as the Western Bulldogs.

1997 Port Adelaide Power join.

2011 Gold Coast Suns join.

2012 Greater Western Sydney (GWS) Giants join.

2020 Major alterations to the traditional 'home-away' season due to the global Covid-19 pandemic. Only 23 games (out of 163) were played in Victoria during this unusual season. The Grand Final was played at The Gabba in Brisbane.

Australian Rules Football player positions – explanation.

In this second edition of the book, I have included the 'Teams of the Century' for all the long-established clubs. You will find them listed at the end of each team chapter. The AFL announced *its* 'Team of the Century' in 1996, during the league's 100th anniversary season. This team is listed near the end of the book. The individual clubs announced their own 'Teams of the Century' soon afterwards. Abbreviations are regularly used to indicate the 18 positions on the field – a clarification of what those abbreviations stand for is below:

B = Backs: = Back Pocket, Full Back, Back Pocket

HB = Half Backs: = Half-Back Flank, Centre Half-Back, Half-Back Flank

C = Centre: = Wing, Centre, Wing

HF = Half Forward: = Half-Forward Flank, Centre Half-Forward, Half-Forward Flank

F = Forwards = Forward Pocket, Full Forward, Forward Pocket

Foll = Followers: = Ruckman, Ruck rover, Rover

Int = Interchange = Interchange bench

Snapshot of the unusual 2020 season

On 11th March the World Health Organization formally confirmed the worldwide Covid-19 pandemic. On 13th March the Melbourne Grand Prix was cancelled only 2 days before the race and the impending AFL season was put into doubt. League officials only announced that the first round would be played at all, one day before the opening match between Richmond-Carlton on 19/3/20. All 9 matches did go ahead that weekend without crowds, but on the Sunday afternoon AFL Commission Chairman Gillon McLaughlin solemnly announced that the season would be immediately suspended due to the pandemic, which had quickly resulted in travel restrictions, social distancing measures, etc being imposed.

Australians are a resilient and resourceful people. The AFL displayed similar qualities in getting the season back on track in June and ensuring it continued virtually uninterrupted through to the Grand Final on 24/10. They, along with club officials & players, are to be loudly applauded for their momentous achievement - it was quite the logistical exercise and many sacrifices had to be made. Here is a summary of a few things that happened during this 'unprecedented' season.

Shorter Season: an 18 round season including a bye round was announced.

Shorter Quarters: 16 minutes plus time-on instead of the usual 20 minutes plus time-on. The idea was to lighten the load on players, given that training schedules would be severely impacted and games were likely to be played closer together than ever before.

Fixtures: when the season resumed in June, rounds 2 to 5 went ahead as originally scheduled. Only one match all year needed to be re-scheduled - the Round 3 fixture between Melbourne-Essendon was played late in the season after the Bombers' Conor McKenna returned a 'false-positive' Covid test. After Round 5 the AFL only released its schedule a few weeks in advance.

A lot of football was played in a short period of time - Rounds 9 to 12 saw 33 matches played over 20 consecutive days. The second period of 'footy frenzy' was between Rounds 14-17 when 31 games were played over 19 days. In some instances, teams had as little as 4 days between matches and in some cases when a team had a 'bye' the rest period between games might be as little as one week (not a fortnight as in previous seasons). I thought the AFL did an incredible job in organizing the fixtures and the players were just as incredible in backing up so quickly during the condensed schedule!

Crowds: due to government restrictions on gatherings, crowds were not permitted to attend any of the Round 1 games in March - the first time in the code's history that this had happened. When the season resumed in June, the state governments of WA, SA, NSW and Queensland permitted small crowds to attend matches. Spectator numbers gradually increased as the season progressed but were still limited even though most states outside of Victoria had relatively low case numbers. An interesting experiment involved broadcasters introducing artificial crowd noise to their telecasts to provide a more 'normal' experience for their viewers.

Quarantine Hubs

The hubs were the key to ensuring that the season could proceed - they helped to keep players and officials as safe as possible and the players/umpires/staff were regularly tested for the virus. Training was quite challenging as it had to be done in very small groups in order to comply with government guidelines. Family members were permitted to stay in the hubs but were subject to the same stringent rules. The guidelines were breached a number of times during the year which resulted in fines for players, clubs and, in the worst situations, the suspension of players. Given the steep challenges faced by the AFL, the clubs, players and their families, I think the hub arrangements worked pretty well. It must have been very difficult for the players to be separated from their families for lengthy periods as happened in 2020. Below is a summary of where/when the hubs were set up.

Rounds 2-6 - the South Australian and West Australian teams were relocated to Queensland. The South Australian teams were able to travel freely between SA-Queensland after Round 6.

Rounds 7-14 - there were 3 three-week hubs in Perth involving Geelong & Collingwood, Hawthorn & Carlton and the Swans & GWS, during which time the interstate teams would play each other one week and play the 2 WA teams on the other two weeks.

Rounds 15-18 - the 2 WA teams returned to their Queensland hubs for the final 4 rounds.

Round 6 onwards - the 10 Victorian teams had to leave their state after Round 5 due to the worsening Covid-19 situation in Melbourne. Initially 6 clubs went to Queensland and 4 to NSW. The NSW hubs involving Collingwood, Hawthorn,

Geelong & Melbourne lasted for 3 weeks only and after Round 8, these 4 teams plus the 2 NSW teams **all** shifted to Queensland hubs. After round 5 no more matches were played in Victoria and after Round 8 there were no further matches in NSW. Three games were played in the Northern Territory and for the first time since 2000, no matches were played in Tasmania. Queensland was ***the*** saviour for the AFL in 2020 and our sport has hopefully attracted many new fans in the Sunshine State - which historically has been mainly rugby territory.

Interesting Outcomes of Season 2020 (163 games in total were played - normally 207 are played).

I was interested to work out where all of the 163 games were played and here is the breakdown, indicating the stadium (state) and number of games hosted.

Metricon Stadium (Qld) - 44; *The Gabba* (Qld) - 36; *Adelaide Oval* (SA) - 22; *Optus Stadium* (WA) - 17; *MCG* (Vic) - 10; *Marvel Stadium* (Vic) - 10; *Giants Stadium* (NSW) - 9; *SCG* (NSW) - 5; *Cazaly's Stadium* (Qld) - 4; *GMHBA Stadium* (Vic) - 3; *Marrara Oval* (NT) - 2; *Traeger Park* (NT) - 1

A very low-scoring season

Modern-day football has a strong emphasis on tight defence and high scoring games are not so common today. Combine this with the fact that the games were about 20% less in duration because of the shorter quarters and it is not surprising that we had some very low scores in Season 2020. Here are a few interesting statistics:

In 44 of the 163 games (fully 27% of the time) a team scored less than 40 points! In ten of these games the losing team scored less than 30 points and in 2 games the losing side didn't even manage 20 points! The round 6 game between Richmond-Sydney saw a paltry *total* of only 60 points scored for the match!

On the flip side, it proved difficult for teams to score 100 points in 2020 - this happened only 8 times all year (a mere 5% of the time). The highest total score for one game by both teams came in Round 9 when bottom of the table teams North Melbourne and Adelaide tallied a combined 169 points.

The 2020 Finals: in the first week of the finals, minor premiers Port Adelaide defeated Geelong and Brisbane had their first win over Richmond since 2009 - both of the victors thereby earned an extra week's rest. St Kilda progressed to the second week, just... after holding on for a 3-point win over the Western Bulldogs. In the other elimination final, Collingwood downed West Coast in Perth, recording a nail-biting, exciting one-point victory! In the week 2 semi-finals it was surprising to see the Magpies lose their game to the Cats by a whopping 68 points. Richmond comfortably accounted for a wayward St Kilda in the other game - the Richmond vs St Kilda game marked only the fourth time that these 2 teams had met in the finals in 113 seasons.

Port Adelaide and Brisbane both entered their respective preliminary finals versus Richmond and Geelong as favourites, having had the extra week's rest. They also had home-ground advantage with about 25,000 spectators attending the Port vs Richmond game at Adelaide Oval and 29,000 on hand to see Brisbane take on Geelong. As things turned out the vast finals' experience of both Richmond and Geelong proved to be the decisive factor. Port Adelaide fought hard but the Tigers got on top in the final term to record a one goal win. In the other Preliminary Final, Brisbane were no match for Geelong and lost by 40 points. It was a disappointing finish for the Lions' supporters who had been so hoping to see their team play in the first Grand Final ever held outside of Victoria, which of course was held on Brisbane's home ground, The Gabba.

The 2020 Grand Final also marked the first time the big game has been played at night. A crowd of 29,707 witnessed history being made on 24/10/20. Geelong held the upper hand for most of the first half and led by 15 points at the main change. In the second half Richmond turned things around, mainly thanks to their super star Dustin Martin, who imposed himself on the game. Dusty kicked 4 telling goals for the match as Richmond kicked away late to record a 31-point win. It was the Tigers' third premiership win in 4 years and Martin became the first player in history to win a third Norm Smith Medal for being voted best on ground in a Grand Final.

Conclusion: during a season which had been like no other, the league and its clubs did a remarkable job. The Covid-19 crisis resulted in major financial losses across the board. Things could have been far worse had the season not resumed in June - the league was at least able to take in most of its TV revenues. Australians love football and during the long winter months of isolation (especially in Victoria) it was wonderful for many people that they could at least watch a lot of footy on TV.

Origin of Australian Rules Football

Evolution of Australian Rules Football in Victoria 1858-1896

The game which became known as Australian Rules Football started in 1858 with a game between Melbourne Grammar - Scotch College which was played over 3 weekends. Tom Wills was keen to find a game which would help keep cricketers fit during the winter - he organized and umpired that first match. Wills, along with William Hammersley, Tom Smith and James Thompson met in May 1859 to write the 10 rules which form the basis of today's game. For about the next 20 years administration of the game including agreement on rules was conducted in an *ad hoc* fashion by participating clubs. The club secretaries would meet on an informal basis from time to time to make decisions. The game evolved as a blend of Gaelic football, rugby and soccer. Some historians think that the indigenous game *Marn Grook*, which featured punt kicking and catching a stuffed ball (and played by up to 100 players) was also an inspiration behind the early development of Australian football. In the very early days teams played on large rectangular-shaped fields with players having to navigate around the trees that dotted those fields and playing with a *round* ball! The game has been evolving for 160+ years and long ago became an important part of Australian culture.

Background to the 1896 VFA-VFL split

In 1877 the Victorian Football Association (VFA) was

established 'to provide formal and binding administration of the game in Victoria'. Meetings of the VFA starting at that time and for many years to come were held at Melbourne's iconic *Young & Jackson's Hotel* at the corner of Flinders & Swanston Streets. The VFA served as both the game's administrative body and as the top senior competition in Victoria... but not for long.

By 1896, there were a few reasons that a number of teams decided to leave the VFA to set up a separate competition. Nine years earlier in 1887, there were 18 teams in the competition and it was considered too big & unwieldy. While the VFA did manage to reduce the number of teams to 13 by the early 1890s (via amalgamations and dropping the 2 Ballarat teams), this was still a large and uneven number. For many years there had been 'issues' with the draw - for the first 15 years after 1877 the draws were *not* done under the auspices of the VFA, rather they were organized by the club secretaries. The top clubs (Essendon, South Melbourne, Melbourne, Fitzroy, Geelong) dominated these discussions and would regularly organize their home games at the start of the season versus the weaker clubs. This gave the top clubs a huge advantage and, put simply, there were far too many uneven games. The *Argus* newspaper wrote in 1893:

"All clubs were supposed to enter the competition for the premiership on equal terms, yet seven out of the thirteen clubs have not only no chance of winning, but only a remote prospect of finishing in the first three... (and) by having a monopoly on the best dates, the top clubs also receive some of the strongest gate takings... for example crowds were generally higher in May when the weather was good than in July when it was colder & wetter."

Tensions also arose between clubs over venues, player poaching & permits, professionalism and distributing gate receipts. Whenever the smaller clubs sought to even out the competition, the top clubs resisted and the VFA was perceived to be slow to step in to resolve the problems.

Ultimately, the main issue was about money. The stronger clubs wanted greater administrative control, commensurate with their relative financial contribution to the game. However, in July 1896 the Secretary of the VFA Mr TS Marshall, responding to requests from the weaker clubs to help make the competition more even, put forward a radical solution. He recommended that "the gross receipts of **all** clubs should be paid into the Association, with the clubs to receive £5 per week... That would give the Association £500, which could be distributed amongst the charities and the clubs would thereby render valuable services to needy persons and at the same time enlist increased patronage from the public."

The reaction of the top clubs to this proposal was predictable - they were not happy. If Marshall's proposal was accepted it would see a great deal of their revenue pass to the Association and with it a lot of their power. Things came to a head pretty quickly. A majority vote of 7 (of the 13 clubs) would be needed to proceed with the recommendation. Instead, what transpired was that the 6 strongest clubs namely Essendon, South Melbourne, Melbourne, Fitzroy, Geelong & Collingwood (who had only joined in 1892 but would win the premiership in 1896) pushed to create a breakaway competition and invited two of the weaker clubs (on the field), namely Carlton & St Kilda, to join them. I was interested to read why Carlton & St Kilda received invitations and why Port Melbourne & North Melbourne did not.

Carlton: they were a bit lucky to get the nod ahead of North

Melbourne. At that stage the Blues were very uncompetitive and didn't have a permanent home ground. They were able to secure a portion of Princes Park to resolve the latter problem and got the invitation because they had always had a strong following including good gate receipts.

St Kilda: did have a good home ground (Junction Oval) with easy access and the new league was keen to have a presence south of the Yarra River. Plus, St Kilda were seen to have maintained their reputation for playing the game upon its merits as a "pastime" - they were seen to embody the 'amateur spirit' and their supporters were regarded as 'the right kind of people' for the new league.

Port Melbourne: their club historian suggests that the club 'had sinned too often' on and off the field, that Port's waterfront characteristics made the dockworkers 'socially undesirable' and that they were geographically located too close to South Melbourne. As I was reading this explanation, I thought it sounded very similar to the reaction to Port Adelaide in the SANFL at about the same time.

North Melbourne: their fate seems to have been sealed as a result of a riot after a Collingwood vs North game at the North Melbourne Recreation Reserve (Arden Street) in July 1896. Many NM fans were incensed with umpire Roberts over his interpretation of the 'little mark' rule after their team lost 4 goals to 5. They invaded the field, including men with iron bars and ladies wielding long hat pins! Players from both teams "...were forced to protect Roberts from the mob... before he was escorted off the ground by police." A North Melbourne player was badly injured after a blow to the head. This disgraceful incident added to the already bad reputation of the North Melbourne ground and the 'ruffianly element' of its patrons and has been cited as a major reason why the *Shinboners* were not invited to join the breakaway league.

Williamstown, Footscray and **Richmond** were the other teams left out in the cold. The departing clubs left the VFA with a lot of debt - it was not an amicable separation. The 5 teams left behind were given the opportunity to compete as a junior competition under and without representation on the VFL's administration, but rejected the offer and continued as an independent body. Both the VFA and the new VFL competition competed in parallel from 1897 onwards, with games played on a Saturday afternoon. Although there were two leagues operating from 1897, it was widely acknowledged from the start that the new VFL was the top competition in Victoria.

Development of the two leagues after the 1896 split

VFL: with the best Victorian teams playing in the new league, the VFL pretty much went from strength to strength throughout the 20th century. When they wanted to expand their competition, the VFL were happy to consider approaches from certain VFA teams. Richmond joined the

VFL in 1908 from the VFA and in 1925, North Melbourne, Footscray and Hawthorn followed.

The other team to join the VFL (2 weeks before Richmond in 1908) was the Melbourne University Team, simply known as **University**. Players for this team had to have matriculated or hold a higher degree to be eligible. It was the only team to be purely amateur as most of the other clubs (except Melbourne) were starting to pay some of their players (not enough to earn a living) from the early 1900s. University ended up losing their last 51 games in a row and withdrew from the league at the end of 1914 after only 7 seasons. A number of their players transferred to the Melbourne FC. World War I had arrived and not all clubs could continue to field a team – in 1916 there were only 4 teams (Carlton, Collingwood, Richmond & Fitzroy). During World War II the only team that was forced to withdraw for two seasons was Geelong in 1942-43.

VFA: in order to resurrect its competition, the VFA added a number of new teams from 1897 including: Brunswick (1897), Prahran (1899), West Melbourne (1899), Essendon Town (1900) and Preston (1903). All of these had been leading junior clubs.

The relationship between the VFA and the VFL remained fractious for a very long time. Players sometimes moved between the two leagues (or were poached) and at various times permit reciprocity agreements were agreed by the two leagues to keep the movement under control. These agreements tended not to last very long.

Having lost three of its stronger teams to the VFL in 1925, the VFA quickly expanded again by adding clubs from Coburg (1925), Camberwell (1926), a new club from Preston (1926), Yarraville (1928), Oakleigh (1929) and Sandringham (1929).

The Schism ('Throw-Pass Era' in the VFA) 1938-49 - an interesting period for our sport!

Background: in 1906 the Australian National Football Council (ANFC) was formed. It would be the national governing body for the sport for the next 90 years (and had a few name changes over this time). It helped to organize interstate matches, promote the game in the rugby states, oversee a system of interstate player transfers and codify the rules of

the game. Unfortunately, the VFA had no representation on this body - the Victorian delegate(s) came from the VFL.
In 1938 the VFA decided to make some major changes to its competition - since they weren't a part of the ANFC, the VFA felt it could act unilaterally and do what it wanted.

Their most significant **new rule** was to legalize passing in general play - similar to rugby the passing had to be done underarm with both hands below shoulder height. The idea was to speed up play and reduce congestion on the field and both these aims were achieved.

Two other rules which the VFA ***modified*** in the late 1930s were:

1. The **holding the ball rule** by eliminating the provision for a player to drop the ball when tackled.
2. Re-introducing the **boundary throw-in** whenever the ball went out of bounds.

The VFA hoped that these changes would give them an on-field product to rival the VFL. In addition to the rule changes, the other thing the VFA did was to start aggressively recruiting some of the top VFL stars by offering salaries well above the maximum set by VFL player payment laws. Big names to move across to the VFA during the Schism (which they could do without a clearance) included Laurie Nash, Bob Pratt, Ron Todd, Des Fothergill, Jack Titus, Herbie Matthews and Harry Vallence, all of whom were considered amongst the finest footballers in the country.

Outcomes: the VFA's bold plans didn't quite work out as they had hoped.

1. While attendance levels at VFA matches did improve significantly thanks to new fans finding the game more appealing, the Association's attendance figures still lagged far behind attendance levels at VFL matches. However, the 1940s is widely accepted as being the VFA's most successful decade since the 1896 split... even though wartime meant that the league went into recess for three seasons between 1942-44.

2. The VFA had hoped that the ANFC would see fit to adopt the throw-pass concept for all competitions but this never happened - amongst the many objections,

there was real concern that Australian Rules might become indistinguishable from rugby if throw-passing was adopted.

3. While the ANFC did not codify the throw-pass, a number of Victorian country leagues and leagues in NW Tasmania ***did*** codify these rules - the concept did have its supporters.

4. The holding the ball rule and boundary throw in rule were immediately adopted by the ANFC in 1939 - these rules have had only minor modifications since and remain an integral part of Aussie Rules football 80 years later.

5. The ANFC spent most of the 1940s attempting to get the VFL and VFA engaged in discussions to agree on a common set of rules. Finally, in 1949 the VFA were promised a seat on the ANFC in return for recognizing a set of uniform rules for the game which ***did not*** include throw-pass. Common sense to have one set of rules eventually prevailed.

The 1950s saw a period of declining attendances in the VFA - with the 'throw-pass' gone, they lost their point of distinction with the VFL. During the 1960s & 1970s the VFA was able to turn its fortunes around a bit by starting to play matches on Sundays, having certain matches shown on TV and expanding to include teams from Melbourne's fast-growing outer suburbs. This prosperity didn't last long and by the 1980s many of their clubs were in dire financial straits.

There also continued to be friction between the VFA and the VFL. After the 1994 season the VFA was formally disbanded as an administrative body and since 2000 teams playing in what was 'the old VFA' merged with the AFL Reserves competition.

Adelaide Crows

♪♫ *"We're the pride of South Australia..."* ♪♫

Background to their entry to the AFL in 1991... rocky beginnings!

Once the VFL started scheduling matches in Sydney from 1979 it was clear that the league hoped to expand its competition beyond Victorian borders. As long ago as 1980 the East Perth club made an approach to the VFL to have their team included in the VFL. About a year later the Norwood Football Club in Adelaide also made an approach and in 1982 the SANFL (South Australian National Football

League) spoke to the VFL about entering a composite team from South Australia. All these approaches were politely declined by the VFL. Their excuse was that they weren't considering national expansion at that time (except to have a team based in Sydney, which happened from 1982). An unstated reason was that the VFL were happy to see their teams continue to recruit the best talent from interstate which in turn strengthened the VFL competition.

By 1986 the VFL's attitude had changed - with some of its own clubs facing serious financial challenges, the league regarded national expansion as the way forward. In 1987 two new teams, the West Coast Eagles & Brisbane Bears joined the VFL but why didn't a team from 'footy-talented' South Australia join at that time? The answer is mainly that the SANFL balked at the high licence fee of $4 million that they would need to pay in 1987 to enter a team that year. The SANFL continued to negotiate with the VFL/AFL over the next few years and in 1990 advised the AFL that they planned to enter a team in 1993. However, the AFL was keen to get a South Australian team on board in time for the 1991 season and didn't want to wait an extra two years.

The AFL was on the verge of admitting the Port Adelaide team (with whom they'd been secretly negotiating) to the AFL in 1991 but when news of Port's approach was made public, the other 9 SANFL Clubs reacted strongly and entered into litigation to stop Port's bid! The upshot of this saga was that the AFL put another proposal to the SANFL to enter a **composite South Australian team** with financial arrangements which were much better than previously offered (licence fee of c. $1.5 million). The SANFL accepted and the Adelaide Crows Football team was formed in time to take the field in 1991.

The SANFL bought the licence fee for Adelaide (and later Port Adelaide) for c. $1.5 mil each time. In 2014 both SA teams (the Crows and Port Power) bought their respective licences back from the SANFL for a combined total of $18 million, spread over 15 years. Each club henceforth reports directly to the AFL Commission (not the SANFL). Further, both Adelaide and Port Adelaide field a local team in the SA Statewide Super League (except in the Covid-19 affected 2020 season) which is effectively the Reserves team for both clubs.

First game: I remember watching on TV as the Crows

smashed Hawthorn by 86 points in the opening round of their inaugural 1991 season at Adelaide's Football Park. Given that the Hawks had appeared in 7 of the previous 8 Grand Finals (and would also win the premiership in 1991) it was a stunning score line. Adelaide finished a creditable 9th in the 15-team league that season.

The Crows only made the finals once during their first 6 years in the AFL – this was in 1993, a year in which their sensational goal kicker Tony Modra booted 129 goals. At half-time during that year's Preliminary Final versus Essendon, Adelaide led by 42 points and looked certain to qualify for the Grand Final against Carlton. It wasn't to be however, as the team fell apart in the second half and lost the game by 11 points.

1997-1998 Premierships: it would be 4 more years before the Crows qualified for the finals but against the odds, they won back-to-back flags under the coaching of Malcolm Blight. In the 1997 preliminary final versus the Western Bulldogs the Crows overcame a 31-point half-time deficit, kicked 4 unanswered goals in the final term and snuck home by 2 points. In the Grand Final versus minor premiers St Kilda,

Adelaide again overcame a half-time deficit, kicking 14 second half goals to win going away by 31 points - overcoming the absence of key players Tony Modra, Mark Ricciuto and Peter Vardy in the process.

In 1998, the Crows finished 5th after the home/away rounds. They lost a qualifying final to the Melbourne Demons at the MCG by a whopping 8 goals, but the finals' system at that time meant they had a second chance. Adelaide made the most of their opportunity and easily beat Sydney at the SCG, before trouncing the Bulldogs at the MCG in the preliminary final to qualify for their second straight GF - this time versus North Melbourne. As had happened the year before, they started slowly and trailed by 4 goals at the half. However, they came out full of running in the second half and steamrolled the Kangaroos to win by 35 points. In both of these Grand Finals, Darren Jarman & Andrew McLeod played starring roles with McLeod winning the Norm Smith Medal both years.

Since the glory days, the Crows have experienced more 'lows' than 'highs' including: being charged with salary cap breaches and draft tampering in 2012; the bizarre stabbing death of their coach Phil Walsh in 2015; the disappointment of badly losing the 2017 GF after being minor premiers that season. On the plus side Adelaide was the first team to exceed 50,000 members in 2006.

Great Indigenous Player

Andrew McLeod

He was born in Darwin and his original team was the Darwin Buffaloes. Fremantle had his rights in the AFL but on the eve of their first season in the competition traded away those rights to the Adelaide Crows in 1994 (no doubt something they later regretted!). McLeod went on to be an absolute superstar for the Crows and is their games' record holder having played 340 games for the club between 1995-2010. He was terrific in the mid-field, at half back or on the forward flank with his pace & agility. The Crows won back-to-back premierships in 1997-98 with McLeod starring in both finals' series and collecting Norm Smith Medals for best on ground in both of those Grand Finals.

Great Goal Kicker

Tony Modra (Adelaide 1992-98, Freo 1999-2001) **588 goals**

Modra was born in McLaren Vale SA and joined the Crows in 1992 in the club's second AFL season. At the start of the 1993 season, he was moved to the full-forward position after the Crows' regular full-forward suffered an injury. He made an immediate impact and had a spectacular year in '93, kicking 129 goals as Adelaide progressed as far as the Preliminary Final. Modra had tremendous agility and was known for his spectacular high-flying marks. He was the club's leading goal kicker for 5 straight years (1993-'97) and won the Coleman Medal in 1997. Sadly, tragedy stuck in that year's Preliminary Final when he suffered an anterior cruciate ligament injury which kept him out of Adelaide's first premiership winning team. He wasn't able to make a return until well into the following season and managed only 8 games in 1998. His form had dropped off and he wasn't selected in the Crows' GF team that beat North Melbourne. He finished his career with Fremantle where he continued to kick a lot of goals before injury forced his retirement.

Showdown Matches – Adelaide vs Port Adelaide

The team has a very fierce rivalry with cross-town rivals Adelaide – matches between the two teams are called ***The***

Showdown, and Malcolm Blight refers to them as 'the greatest rivalry in football'. After 48 Showdown matches the ledger stands at 24 wins for each team! There are usually 2 Showdown matches each season.

Some history - why are these matches so intense?

South Australians take their football very seriously and their fans are very passionate/parochial. Back in 1990 as a result of their secret negotiations with the AFL, Port were expecting to be admitted to the AFL as the new South Australian team the following year. At the same time the Norwood FC (Port's bitter rivals in the SANFL) were also negotiating directly with the AFL to try to get *their* team admitted. The recently re-branded AFL was speaking to both of these teams separately because the SANFL were taking too long to commit to entering a South Australian side in the AFL. Port's bid was blocked in court and finally the SANFL 'came to the party' and quickly created a composite SA team. While Port Adelaide was awarded the second SA licence, they had to wait 6 extra years before their team could join the AFL. Given these circumstances it is hardly surprising that matches between the two clubs are played with a lot of feeling! The pride of South Australia is at stake!

The Showdown is fun because you can expect the unexpected - ladder rankings are not a good indicator of which team will likely win. Over the years the team which was lower on the ladder has won the game about 1/3 of the time. The overall head-to-head differential between the two clubs has never been greater than 6 and they are currently level on wins after 24 years of head to head games! The teams have only met one another in the finals on one occasion – a Semi-Final played at Football Park in 2005 which Adelaide won by 83 points!

Some further Showdown stats

Closest Adelaide win: 3 points in 2015 and 2018
Biggest Adelaide win: 84 points in 2017
Closest Port Adelaide win: 4 points in 2013
Biggest Port Adelaide win: 75 points in 2020

Showdown Medal: a medal has been awarded since the 2000 season to the player adjudged to be best on ground. The following players have won this award on multiple occasions. Adelaide: Mark Ricciuto (3), Sam Jacobs (3), Simon Goodwin

(2)

Port Adelaide: Robbie Gray (5), Josh Francou (3), Travis Boak (2)

Adelaide's Silver Anniversary Team (1991-2015)

B: *Ben Hart, Ben Rutten, Michael Doughty*

HB: *Nigel Smart, Nathan Bock, Andrew McLeod*

C: *Simon Goodwin, Scott Thompson, Richard Douglas*

HF: *Bernie Vince, Matthew Robran, Tyson Edwards*

F: *Darren Jarman, Tony Modra, Brett Burton*

Foll: *Shaun Rehn, Mark Ricciuto (Capt), Tony McGuinness*

Int: *Mark Bickley, Nathan Bassett, Gordon Johncock, Chris McDermott*

Coach *Malcolm Blight*

Brisbane Lions

♪♪ *"We are the pride of Brisbane town..."* ♪♪

Incorporating the Brisbane Bears & Fitzroy Lions

The club was formed at the end of 1996 as a result of the merger between the Brisbane Bears and Fitzroy Lions football clubs.

In 1999 Leigh Matthews was recruited to coach the Lions and he made an immediate impact. In his first season the team finished 4th, a huge improvement from their wooden spoon status the year before. In the early 2000s, the Lions dominated and won 3 straight premierships from 2001-03. They were slight favourites to make it 4 in a row the following year but were overrun by Port Adelaide in the second half of the Grand Final. The Lions' galaxy of stars during their golden era included Michael Voss, Jason Akermanis, Simon Black (all Brownlow medallists), Justin Leppitsch, Shaun Hart and Jonathan Brown.

The club plays its home games at The Gabba (the ground is situated in the Brisbane suburb of Woolloongabba) and for the last 2 years has had a membership of just under 30,000. Since 2011 a local rivalry with the other southeast Queensland AFL team the Gold Coast Suns has developed – games between these two sides are known as the **QClash**. The Marcus Ashcroft Medal is awarded to the best on ground performer in these matches - Ashcroft was the first Queenslander to play more than 300 games in the AFL registering 318 games for the Brisbane Bears/Brisbane Lions between 1989-2003.

Since 2004, the Lions have experienced a lot of lean years with only one finals' appearance (in 2009) until 2019. In season 2019 the club took a big step forward - jumping from

15th in 2018 to finish 2nd after the home/away rounds (before bowing out in straight sets in the finals). In the Covid-impacted season of 2020, they again finished 2nd on the ladder after the 18 home & away rounds and progressed to a Preliminary Final where they lost to Geelong. Their Tasmanian coach Chris Fagan has the club headed in the right direction. Fagan is not so widely known to Victorian fans as his 263-game playing career was entirely in Tasmania. He was a successful assistant coach at both Melbourne and Hawthorn, helping guide Melbourne to the 2000 Grand Final and Hawthorn to 4 premierships as assistant to Alastair Clarkson. Fagan is contracted to the Lions until the end of 2021.

Fitzroy Lions (1883-1996)

♪♪ "*We are the boys from Old Fitzroy...*" ♪♪

The club was formed in late 1883 and the VFA made a change to its rules to allow Fitzroy immediate entry (as the league's 7th team) into the competition starting the following year. The new team was quickly competitive and duly won a VFA premiership (1895) prior to being one of the breakaway clubs to form the new VFL competition in 1897. For the first 25 years of the VFL Fitzroy were the league's strongest team, amassing 7 premierships between 1898-1922.

Nickname: until the 1930s the club was known as the 'Maroons'. Their nickname then became the 'Gorillas' (sounds unlikely) until 'Lions' was adopted from 1957. They were also frequently referred to as the 'Roy Boys'.

Declining fortunes: Fitzroy's form fell away after they won their 7th flag in 1922. They did manage an 8th flag in 1944 but that would be their final senior premiership. Fitzroy's trajectory in the post-World War II years took a path quite similar to that of South Melbourne. The club didn't make the finals very often (only 4 times between 1945-1978), yet still produced some great individual players (Kevin Murray, Alan Ruthven & Bernie Quinlan won Brownlow medals). More worryingly, by the start of the 1980s and just like South Melbourne, Fitzroy found itself heavily in debt. The club did have a few good years between 1979-86, making the finals 5 times and reaching the preliminary final in 1986. Unfortunately, this period of on-field success didn't translate to more members or greater financial security.

Home Ground: compounding the club's woes in the 1960s was the deteriorating state of their home ground at

Brunswick Street (which they shared with the local cricket club). Unfortunately, a way forward to upgrade the venue and extend their lease could not be found and after 82 years the Lions were forced to relocate at the end of 1966. For the next 30 years Fitzroy led a nomadic existence playing 'home games' at Princes Park, Junction Oval, Victoria Park, Princes Park (again) and finally the Western Oval. Similarly, their training and administrative bases also moved around a fair bit - it was hard to attract top players with so many changes happening and no secure 'home base'.

The years 1980-1996

In July 1980 Fitzroy club president Frank Bibby, publicly stated that his club was effectively bankrupt and that he proposed moving the team to Sydney! I was astounded to read of the number of mergers and relocations that were variously proposed/considered for Fitzroy between 1980 and 1996 when they finally did merge with the Brisbane Bears. Below is the chronology.

1980: proposed that Fitzroy relocate to Sydney where they would become known as the Sydney Lions - after 1200 members met in August and a fund-raising campaign was launched to keep the team in Melbourne, the relocation idea was quashed and Bibby resigned.

1986: during this year Fitzroy's finances were so shaky it was rumoured that the club would fold at the end of the season. During that year 2 private consortiums made bids to take control of the club and relocate it to Brisbane and a third consortium proposed moving the team to Canberra. In addition, the club was also investigating a possible merger with either Melbourne, St Kilda or Richmond! None of these discussions came to fruition but thanks to Hecron Pty Ltd stepping up to provide major sponsorship for Fitzroy and pay off some of the debts, the club survived in Melbourne for another decade.

1989: Fitzroy Bulldogs: at the end of the 1989 season the VFL actually announced that a new club would debut the following year and it would be debt-free to start with as the VFL agreed to clear the debts of both Footscray and Fitzroy. The Footscray faithful immediately rallied to raise sufficient money and also found new sponsors, thereby saving their team from extinction. The merger collapsed.

1994: Melbourne & Fitzroy again discussed a merger. Partly due to the failure of a meeting of minds on the naming of a new club, this merger did not get up. Fitzroy also briefly spoke with Hawthorn about a potential merger. Victorian clubs were partly scared off because Fitzroy lacked a permanent training venue and had limited resources to make any merged club a strong entity.

1996: Fitzroy was placed into administration during the season and it was now clear the club could not play on. Merger talks with North Melbourne were well advanced to form a combined club called the North Fitzroy Kangaroos Football Club to commence the following year. The proposal did not go ahead, due to disagreements on the composition of the new club board and partly because North insisted on having a list of 54 players for the following season (which the other AFL Clubs would not accept).

The Brisbane Bears had also put a merger proposal to Fitzroy which the administrator accepted when the North proposal fell through. The merger went ahead however, without giving the Brisbane Bears' members a vote on the matter. Many Brisbane supporters are still unhappy with the way their club handled the merger and this is exacerbated by the club's reluctance to acknowledge the Bears' history despite its clear willingness to regularly acknowledge that of Fitzroy. This has created significant angst, particularly in Melbourne, between long-standing Brisbane supporters and the small number of former Fitzroy supporters who chose to support the new club after Fitzroy went into administration.

Fitzroy's Team of the Century

B: *Bill Stephen, Fred Hughson, Frank Curcio*
HB: *Kevin Murray (Capt), Paul Roos, Gary Pert*
C: *Wilfred Smallhorn, John Murphy, Warwick Irwin*
HF: *Owen Abrahams, Bernie Quinlan, Garry Wilson*
F: *Allan Ruthven, Jack Moriarty, Norm Brown*
Foll: *Alan Gale, Norm Johnstone, Haydn Bunton Sr*
Int: *Michael Conlan, Alastair Lynch, Harvey Merrigan, Richard Osborne, Percy Parratt, Percy Trotter*
Coach *Len Smith*

Brisbane Bears(1987-1996)

♪♫ "*Dare to beat the Bear...*" ♪♫

The Bears were one of two new teams (along with West Coast) to join the VFL in time for the 1987 season. The previous year the VFL Commission had announced its intention to expand the competition via the sale of 2 multi-million-dollar licences. The Brisbane licence was awarded to a private consortium headed by former actor Paul Cronin and bankrolled by entrepreneur Christopher Skase.

As there was no suitable ground in Brisbane, the team played its home games exclusively at Carrara Stadium on the Gold Coast for the first 5 years before shifting to Brisbane and playing their home games exclusively at The Gabba from 1993 onwards. The team's inaugural coach was former Hawthorn champion Peter Knights. For most of their ten years the club struggled on the field and financially. Average membership numbers were only about 6,000 and game-day spectator numbers were less than 10,000 in most years. The AFL stepped in to help ensure the club's survival and in both 1995 and 1996, the Bears' on-field performances had improved such that they qualified for the finals in both years - reaching the preliminary final in their final season.

Great Indigenous Player

Darryl White (Brisbane)

White has been a true role model for indigenous Australians for many years. He had a distinguished 14-year career with Brisbane between 1992-2005 and was a triple premiership player for the Lions. He won goal of the year honours in 1992. White could jump very high and took a number of spectacular marks during his career. He was mainly used in defence but because of his great leap and sure hands, was moved to other positions to help the team. He initially found the move from Alice Springs to Brisbane a difficult one, under hard task-master coach Robert Walls. At one training session which involved an 8 km cycle up a mountain, White hurled his bike off a cliff, telling his coach he had come to Brisbane to play football, not ride bikes!

Great Coach

Leigh Matthews Coached 20 seasons (10 – Collingwood, 10 – Brisbane), 4 premierships (1 Collingwood, 3 Brisbane), inaugural legend of AFL Hall of Fame in 1996.

He had a decorated 332 game playing career with Hawthorn (1969-85), winning 4 flags. After a successful decade coaching Collingwood, Matthews joined the Lions as coach in 1999 and led the team to 3 consecutive premierships between 2001-03.

Great Goal Kickers

Jack Moriarty (Essendon, Fitzroy 1922-33) **662 goals**

After only one season with Essendon, he crossed to Fitzroy where he had an outstanding 10-year career with the Maroons. Despite his diminutive stature (177 cm, 60 kgs), he had the ability to jump high over opponents and take strong marks. Led the league with 82 goals in 1924 - setting a league record in the process.

Bernie Quinlan (Footscray & Fitzroy, 1969-86) **817 goals**

'Superboot' was a prodigious kick who was the first player to play over 150 games for two clubs! At Footscray he was mainly used as a centre-half forward but sometimes played at centre-half back. The Bulldogs were struggling financially during the 1970s and were forced to clear some of their better players to other clubs (Fitzroy paid $70,000 in 1978 to secure his services). In 1979 Quinlan announced to the club that he planned to return to work on his farm but when the team offered him a substantial pay increase, he relented and stayed for another 7 seasons until retiring after the 1986 season. By that point he had helped lead the Lions to their most successful post-war period and he became the club's first (and still their only) century goal kicker! I was very lucky to be visiting Melbourne in August 1983, attending the Round 21 match between Fitzroy-Collingwood at the Junction Oval on the day that Quinlan notched his 100th goal! He booted over 100 the following year as well and won the Coleman Medal both times. In 1981 Quinlan was a co-winner of the Brownlow Medal with South Melbourne's Barry Round - both players had started their careers with Footscray in the late 1960s!

Alastair Lynch (Fitzroy, Brisbane Bears, Brisbane Lions 1988-2004) **633 goals**

Lynch spent most of his early years with Fitzroy playing in defence – at 193 cm tall, he was an intimidating presence in the Fitzroy backline. In his final year at Fitzroy, coach Robert Shaw shifted him to full-forward where he responded by kicking 68 goals in 1993. Not long after moving to the Bears he contracted a 'mystery illness' which was later diagnosed to be chronic fatigue syndrome. The illness limited his playing time during the next 4 seasons. Lynch was widely applauded for overcoming chronic fatigue and when Leigh Matthews arrived to coach the Lions in 1999, he helped Lynch develop into one of the most feared full-forwards in the league. Lynch was a key member of the Lions' triple premiership teams between 2001-03, averaging 70 goals/year during that period.

Jonathan Brown (Brisbane Lions 2000-2014) **594 goals**

One of the league's marquee centre-half forwards, Brown joined the Lions in 2000 and won 3 premiership medallions early in his career. At 195 cms, he was an imposing target at centre-half forward. His best years were 2006-07. Brown started 2006 in sensational form, displaying impressive aerial skills and accuracy in front of goal. Unfortunately, he was injured in Round 10 and took no further part in that year's competition - in those first 10 games Brown polled 13 Brownlow votes! The following year in 2007 he remained injury-free, won the Coleman Medal and was selected to the All-Australian team. Brown had the honour of being the Lions' captain between 2009-12 and was inducted into the AFL Hall of Fame in 2020.

Carlton Blues

♪♫ "*We are the Navy Blues...*" ♪♫

Never far from success and controversy!

The Carlton Footy Club is one of the country's oldest, founded in 1864. Its administrative and training headquarters are located at Princes Park, where the club played its home games between 1897-2005. The club grew its supporter base very quickly in the 1860s & '70s and had a very keen rivalry with the Melbourne FC in the early years of competition. The Blues also boasted one of the game's early super stars in

George Coulthard - he played six seasons for the club before tragically dying of tuberculosis in 1883 at the age of 27. Coulthard was one of the Blues' leaders when they won the first ever VFA premiership in 1877.

Carlton were in decline in the 1890s to the early 1900s until Jack Worrall joined the club as coach. Under his leadership the club not only won three flags in a row (1906-1908), they were on a sound financial footing - the Blues enticed a number of top players from other clubs to join Carlton. By going through the 1908 season with only 1 loss the club set a standard which still stands today and which has only been equalled by Collingwood in 1929 and Essendon in 2000 - only 1 loss for the entire year.

Despite the success under Worrall, trouble wasn't far away! By 1909 some players became frustrated by low payments and hard training standards and responded by refusing to train or even play matches! Worrall was removed as coach part way through the '09 season and some of the players loyal to him departed too. In 1910 several players were suspected of taking bribes to fix matches - 2 of them were found guilty and each was suspended for 99 matches!

Despite the turmoil Carlton were good enough to make it to the 1909 & '10 Grand Finals and then in 1914-15 with a revamped and largely inexperienced list, claimed back to back flags.

The years between the two World Wars saw Carlton play in many finals' matches but it took a long 23 years before they tasted premiership success again in 1938. A few years later under Percy Bentley the club won flags in 1945 and 1947 before falling back - the 1950s through to 1964 was the club's worst spell since the 1890s. Carlton's fortunes turned when George Harris became president in late 1964 and recruited Melbourne's Ron Barassi to cross to the Blues as the team's captain-coach. During the 22-year period from 1967-1988 the Blues only missed the finals 3 times, contested 10 Grand Finals and won 7 premierships.

Despite the team's on-field success, the '70s & '80s saw its share of off-field instability. Between 1975-1981 the club had 6 different coaches including John Nicholls, Ian Thorogood, Ian Stewart, Alex Jesaulenko, Percy Jones and David Parkin. When George Harris was replaced by Ian Rice as president in early 1980, Jezza and a number of other Harris/Jezza supporters left the club. Yet on the field the club thrived and led by top calibre players like Bruce Doull, Wayne Johnston, Mike Fitzpatrick, Peter Bosustow and Ken Hunter, the team won consecutive flags in 1981-82. Their 14th flag in 1982 was a milestone in that they surpassed Collingwood in having won the highest number of premierships - a record they still co-hold today with Essendon (16 flags).

Flamboyant John Elliott became club president in 1983 and would remain for 20 seasons. The Blues won two more flags in '87 and '95 under the captaincy of Stephen Kernahan, but the club was starting to struggle financially by the late '90s due to some unwise financial investments by Elliott. The construction of a new grand stand at Princes Park came at a heavy cost - at the time many other clubs were finding it more profitable to play their games at the central venues like the MCG or the new Docklands Stadium. Much worse was to come. At the end of the 2002 season it was revealed that Carlton had been systematically cheating the league's salary cap rules for several seasons. The club was penalized with the loss of future draft picks and fined $930,000.00. This scandal saw Elliott voted out as president by the members after the 2002 season. The club has been struggling ever since. Once priding themselves on having 'never won a wooden spoon' as well as having won the most premierships, Carlton have collected a number of wooden spoons since 2002 and haven't made it to the finals very often. There have been regular coaching changes but nothing much has worked in recent seasons. Fans are hoping that second-year coach David Teague can make a difference.

Great Coaches

Jack Worrall 'The First recognized VFL coach' Coached 18 seasons, 279 games, 59% winning average. (Carlton 8 years for 3 premierships, Essendon 10 years for 2 premierships).

He was one of Australia's great all-round sports' people of the late 19th century, being captain of Fitzroy in the VFA for 6 seasons and also playing for the club's cricket side. He was regarded as a more consistent footballer but after retiring from footy in 1894 continued to play cricket at the elite level, including playing 11 Test matches for Australia. He switched allegiances to join the Carlton Cricket Club in 1896 and finally finished his cricket playing career in 1902 at age 40. He was appointed secretary of the Carlton Football Club in 1902 and immediately set about leading training sessions, instructing players, formulating tactics and recruiting talent in a manner that created the role of club coach that is recognised today. For a number of years, he was often referred to as the club's "manager" or "secretary", until the term "coach" came into common usage. After retiring from coaching Worrall became a successful journalist in the 1920s & '30s.

Percy Bentley Coached 22 seasons coaching Richmond & Carlton. 61% winning record in 414 games. Three premierships, 1 with Richmond, 2 with Carlton.

He was a strong ruckman and great tactician during his 16-year playing career with Richmond (1925-1940). Was captain-coach of the Tigers' 1934 premiership winning team. He moved to Carlton as coach between 1941-1955 and coached the Blues to two flags in 1945 and 1947.

Ron Barassi Coached 23 seasons, 4 clubs (Carlton, North Melbourne, Melbourne, Sydney), 4 premierships, AFL Hall of Fame legend.

His name is synonymous with Australian Rules football and

he is still recognized by many as the game's greatest identity. After being lured to Carlton in late 1964, Barassi quickly established his credentials as a coach. He was the Blues' playing captain-coach until 1969 and led the team to 3 straight Grand Final appearances (for 2 wins) between 1968-70. He left the Blues after the 1971 season to concentrate on his business career.

David Parkin Coached 23 seasons, 3 clubs (Hawthorn, Carlton, Fitzroy), 4 premierships, AFL Hall of Fame, Carlton Coach of the Century.

His greatest successes as a coach came during his two stints with Carlton (1981-'85 and 1991-2000). Parkin led the Blues to premierships in 1981, '82 and 1995. He also took Fitzroy to a preliminary final in 1986, the best result for the Roy Boys since their last flag in 1944! He was one of the first coaches to recognize the importance of closely analysing the strengths/weaknesses of the opposition - something which is taken for granted today. Post-football he has become a well-known media personality.

Great Goal Kickers

Harry Vallence (Carlton 1926-38) **722 goals**

He had a stellar career with the Blues between 1926-36 and represented Victoria on 4 occasions. He was the league's leading goal kicker in 1931 but had a falling out with the club in 1936 after going interstate to represent Victoria. Upon his return he found that he had been demoted to the 'twos' to play centre half-back! He moved to Williamstown in the VFA as their captain-coach the following year. Fortunately, he was lured back to the Blues for the 1938 season, when he helped lead the team to their first premiership win since 1915. However, he moved back to Williamstown for a further three seasons from 1939-41. During this time, he won a VFA premiership (1939) and in May 1941 booted 20 goals versus Sandringham, bringing his total number of goals in both the VFL/VFA to over 1000.

Stephen Kernahan (Carlton 1986-1997) **738 goals**

A South Australian native, Kernahan was initially signed by

the Blues in 1981, but didn't join the club until 1986. He had a glittering 5-year career with Glenelg (1981-'85) in the SANFL, leading them to the 1985 premiership. He made an immediate impact upon joining the Blues in 1986 and after only 1 season, was appointed as club captain at the age of 23. He was highly regarded in this role for the next 11 seasons and holds the record amongst all AFL clubs of 226 games as club captain for one club. Kernahan topped the Blues' goal-kicking list 11 times in his career and he overtook Harry Vallence in his final season to become Carlton's all-time leading goal kicker. He represented South Australia 16 times in inter-state matches and is a member of the AFL Hall of Fame.

Great Indigenous Player

Syd Jackson (East Perth, Carlton, Glenelg)

After a distinguished 5-year career with East Perth, Jackson was recruited by Ron Barassi and joined Carlton in 1969. He was a talented player who usually played in the centre or on the half-forward flank. In a distinguished 8-year career with the Blues he won two premiership medals in 1970 & '72.

Interesting story: Jackson was lucky to play in the 1970 decider after being reported for striking Collingwood's Lee Adamson in the second-semi. He likely would have been outed for several weeks but the tribunal accepted Carlton's defence (devised by Blues' president George Harris with Jackson's approval) that his infraction was in response to a racial taunt. The tribunal exonerated Jackson who took his place in Carlton's team on Grand Final day. Twenty-two years later, Jackson admitted that there had been no racial provocation!

1945 'Bloodbath' Grand Final: Carlton 15.13.103 defeated South Melbourne 10.15.75

This infamous match between South Melbourne - Carlton was played in front of 63,000 spectators at Princes Park (hard to imagine so many people could squeeze in!). It was the game's darkest day. Fists & elbows were flying on and off the field, with players & spectators knocked senseless! Ten players were reported and there should have been more reports. The game was an absolute disgrace which shook the football community to its core (and I expect the wider community as well).

Carlton vs Richmond Rivalry

The two clubs have had a long-standing rivalry based on geographic proximity and large supporter bases. Carlton was a founding member of the old VFL in 1897, while Richmond didn't join the league from the VFA until 1908. In the first half of the 20th century Richmond defeated Carlton twice in Grand Finals in 1921 and again in 1932.

Since 2008 the AFL has seen fit to stage the opening match of the season between these two clubs - a Thursday night fixture at the MCG which usually attracts a crowd of about 80,000 spectators. Matches between the two teams are regarded as 'blockbusters' - regardless of where they are on the ladder a large crowd can be expected. Richmond have completely dominated the head to head clashes in recent years and have not lost a game to Carlton since the 2013 elimination final. It is safe to say however, that there has been no match between Richmond-Carlton since the 1982 Grand Final that has been of genuine significance in terms of the race for the finals or the premiership.

Between 1967-1982 virtually **all matches** between Carlton-Richmond were major fixtures with the result likely to have a bearing on the final outcome of the season!

1967-1982 – a golden era for the Blues and the Tigers

In the two decades preceding 1967 both teams had struggled and finals' appearances were rare. When fortunes changed, the change happened quickly and dramatically. During this 16 year stretch Carlton appeared in 8 Grand Finals (winning 6) while Richmond had 7 GF appearances for 5 wins - an excellent strike rate for both teams. They met one another in the premiership decider on 4 occasions (fully 25% of the time), with each team winning twice.

Carlton had been in the doldrums all through the 1950s and into the '60s. In 1964 the Blues had one of their worst seasons (to that stage) ... finishing 10th in the 12-team competition. At the end of '64 new club president George Harris signed Melbourne legend Ron Barassi to cross to the Blues as player/coach starting in 1965. It was a master stroke. The transfer rocked the football world and remains to this day as one of the biggest player-transfers in our game's history. Barassi's influence soon brought the Blues success when they won their first flag in 21 years by edging Essendon in the 1968 Grand Final. (The final score line of 7.14.56 to 8.5.53 marked the only time that the losing team had kicked more goals in a Grand Final).

In 1966 **Richmond** brought in one of their former players Tom Hafey as coach. Hafey had been coaching successfully in Shepparton for a number of years and his impact at senior VFL level was almost immediate. 'T-shirt Tommy' quickly brought fitness and discipline to the club and during his 11 seasons at the helm, the Tigers won 4 premierships. It is not surprising that Hafey was named Richmond's 'Coach of the Century'. The Tigers had a 'kick long' and 'score often' approach. In 1967 they broke through for their first premiership since 1943 with a close, exciting win over Geelong.

Memorable Finals' Matches

1969 Grand Final Richmond 12.13.85 defeated Carlton 8.12.60

Richmond only squeaked in to the final 4 in '69 by winning

their last 4 games and ousting Hawthorn on percentage - each team finishing with 13 wins for the season. The Tiges certainly peaked at the right time and became only the third team to win the flag from 4th position. They swept through the finals, first demolishing Geelong by 118 pts in the elimination final, then ousting minor premiers Collingwood in the prelim. Defending champs Carlton entered the Grand Final as warm favourites having had the extra week's rest. The Blues rallied from 22 points down at the half to lead by 4 at the final change but the effort to overcome the deficit took a toll. Richmond finished over the top of them in the final quarter - Billy Barrot was the star for Richmond in this game. Have a look at You Tube to see one spectacular goal he kicked that day from way out on the boundary line!

1972 Second Semi Richmond 8.13.61 drew with Carlton 8.13.61

This game was one of few really close games between these two sides during this era. It was a scrappy affair at VFL Park and a replay was required the following week. Richmond thumped Carlton by 41 points in the replay to move straight into the Grand Final. I checked a few of the match results from this era and was interested to see that first one team would win comfortably, then in the next match the other team would return the favour. An interesting statistic is that in the four Grand Finals featuring these two teams between 1969-1982, the underdog won each time!

1972 Grand Final Carlton 28.9.177 defeated Richmond 22.18.150

This ridiculously high-scoring match set a record for total points in a GF that still stands almost 50 years later (the 327 total points scored is unlikely to be bettered anytime soon)! Carlton ruckman/coach John Nicholls masterminded Richmond's downfall in this game. Nicholls had taken over as coach after Barassi left (following the 1971 season) and scored 6 goals that day. Robert Walls also kicked 6 while Alex Jesaulenko tallied 7. Incredibly, the Blues had scored 114 points by halftime, led by 54 points at three quarter time and could coast to victory in the final term. Neil Balme kicked 5 goals for Richmond in a losing cause. Remarkably for a team of Richmond's quality the 1972 GF saw them concede the most points they had ***ever*** conceded in their history to that stage. However, their losing score of 150 points also equalled the highest score ever previously scored in a Grand Final. It must have been an amazing game to witness in person!

1973 Grand Final Richmond 16.20.116 defeated Carlton 12.14.86

Carlton were pre-game favourites after defeating Richmond in the Qualifying Final but the Tigers were desperate to reverse the previous year's result. They adopted a very physical approach. At the 4-minute mark Richmond defender Laurie Fowler hit John Nicholls with a high shirt front which left the towering ruckman lying motionless on the ground for about 3 minutes! A hush fell over the crowd at this scary sight. Nicholls stayed out there but was pretty much dazed for the rest of the game, unable to effectively direct his team. Neil Balme king hit Geoff Southby in the second half and punched Vin Waite. Carlton were roughed up and down for the count. The Blues did not recover. The Tigers had entered the game with their champions Royce Hart and Francis Bourke under injury clouds but in winning the premiership cup ensured that it was an especially grand day for their faithful after their Under 19s and Reserves teams also won.

1982 Grand Final Carlton 14.19.103 defeated Richmond 12.13.85

Once again, these two teams met in two finals matches this year and once again the team with the easier path to the decider lost the big game. Richmond won the second semi comfortably by 23 points earning a week's rest. Carlton had to play Hawthorn in the prelim to earn a rematch with the Tigers. In the first 5 minutes of the GF as light rain fell, Carlton slammed on 3 quick goals to lead by 18 points - which was precisely their winning margin at game's end. Richmond recovered from their shaky start to lead by 11 points at the main change but the Blues took control in the third quarter - the premiership quarter as their coach David Parkin liked to say. This game is well-remembered because of the streaker who ran naked onto the pitch (and very close to Bruce Doull) during the third quarter!

The 1982 Grand Final marked the end of Richmond's golden era. They immediately nosedived after that and for the next 30 years only rarely made the finals.
The Blues continued to be a strong team through the 1980s and won two more premierships in 1987 and again in 1995 to take their league leading tally to 16 (equalled by Essendon

in 2000). Alas for everyone connected with the club, Carlton have been really struggling since 2002. There have been a number of coaching changes over the last 20 years but the team has remained uncompetitive. A return to the glory days still seems a long way off.

Carlton's Team of the Century

B: *Bruce Comben, Stephen Silvagni, Geoff Southby*

HB: *John James, Bert Deacon, Bruce Doull*

C: *Garry Crane, Greg Williams, Craig Bradley*

HF: *Wayne Johnston, Stephen Kernahan (Capt), Alex Jesaulenko*

F: *Ken Hands, Harry Vallence, Rod Ashman*

Foll: *John Nicholls, Sergio Silvagni, Adrian Gallagher*

Int: *Robert Walls, Mike Fitzpatrick, Ken Hunter, Trevor Keogh*

Coach *David Parkin*

Collingwood Magpies

♪♫ "*Good old Collingwood forever...*" ♪♫

Love 'em or hate 'em, there is no denying that the Collingwood Football Club has long been a very successful club. Consider the following: their matches regularly attract the highest attendance figures and highest TV ratings of all the AFL clubs. Since their formation in 1892 they have appeared in a record 44 VFL/AFL Grand Finals (including replays) for 15 victories, 2 draws and 27 losses. Their club song 'Good Old Collingwood Forever' has stood the test of time since 1906 and is the oldest club song in the league. They have an overall winning record against all the long-established clubs and only have a 'losing' record against one club... the West Coast Eagles. They are still the only club to have won four premierships in a row (1927-30). They are the only club to have gone through the home & away rounds undefeated – a record of 18-0 in 1929 before losing the second-semi to Richmond but then bouncing back to comfortably win the Grand Final.

Why are they disliked so much? Non-Collingwood supporters tend to dislike the Magpies more intensely than they do other clubs. The dislike of the club by outsiders is said to have originated during the 1920s and 1930s. During these years the Magpies won 6 flags from 13 Grand Final appearances and their success drew the envy and resentment of other clubs. In this period, Collingwood was also perceived as a Catholic and Irish club, at a time when these groups were looked down upon by the rest of Australian society and subjected to a considerable degree of social exclusion. In the 32 year 'Colliwobble' period between 1958-1990, many non-Collingwood supporters took delight in seeing the club lose 8 Grand Finals - a number of them by narrow margins.

Memorable Day: on 6th October 1990 the 'Pies finally broke the drought when they clobbered the Bombers by 8 goals in the Grand Final. Tony Shaw won the Norm Smith Medal and Peter Daicos kicked one of his freakish goals in this game. The outpouring of joy amongst the army of Collingwood supporters could be felt around the city! It was quite something.

Rivalries: the club has keen rivalries with many clubs! Their longest-term rivalry has been with neighbouring Carlton. No matter where these teams are sitting on the ladder, a huge crowd can be expected when they play one another. Collingwood have won most of their head-to-head-games in the last 18 seasons. The team also has a keen rivalry with Essendon, particularly since the introduction of the ANZAC Day matches in 1995. Over the last 20 years strong rivalries have evolved with the Brisbane Lions and West Coast Eagles and their historic rivalry with Geelong has been re-kindled.

Eddie Maguire was elected president of the club in 1998 and helped put Collingwood on a really sound financial footing.

They were one of the last clubs to abandon their traditional home ground when they moved their home games from Victoria Park to the MCG in 2000. The club has had longevity with coaches compared to most other teams. Nathan Buckley has been at the helm since 2012. He was preceded by Mick Malthouse who had a 12-year stint. Leigh Matthews was coach for 10 seasons and going way back, the legendary Jock McHale for 38 seasons.

The 'Pies came awfully close to winning the premiership in 2018 but narrowly lost to West Coast. In the unusual 2020 season, they were probably hit harder by injuries to key players than all other clubs but still made the finals. They had a thrilling one-point win over West Coast in an Elimination Final in Perth before a loss to Geelong in a Semi-Final ended their charge in 2020.

ANZAC Day Games

Anzac Day has been a very important occasion for over 100 years and from the 1920s to 1959, **no** VFL matches were conducted on 25th April. It took an Act of Parliament in 1960 to allow matches to be played on this solemn day. The first two games to be played on Anzac Day after the restrictions were lifted took place on Monday 25th April 1960 with Fitzroy playing Carlton at Brunswick Street and St Kilda playing Melbourne at the Junction Oval.

If ANZAC day fell on a weekday, between 2-3 matches were usually scheduled, with some of the gate receipts being handed over to the RSL. Over the years prior to 1995, there were several ANZAC Day games which attracted very large crowds - most notably the Carlton vs Essendon clash at VFL Park in 1975 (77,000+) and the Richmond vs Collingwood game at the MCG in 1977 (92,000+). The VFL even scheduled a double-header on ANZAC Day in 1986 at the MCG. This experiment didn't work due to major logistical problems, nor did it attract many spectators - a total of 'only' 40,000 fans for the two games between Melbourne-Sydney and North Melbourne-Geelong.

Sheedy has an idea: while pottering in his garden in 1994, then long-serving Essendon coach Kevin Sheedy started thinking, 'How could football honour those who served, including the legendary Anzacs of World War 1 in the best way possible?' At the time interest in and attendance at ANZAC Day activities was growing. Sheedy's vision was to have an annual game on ANZAC Day between Essendon &

Collingwood. Officials from both clubs met and included RSL President Bruce Ruxton in their meeting. The concept was then worked through with the AFL and the following year the first ANZAC Day clash between these two giants of the league took place in front of a crowd of 94,825 (second largest home & away attendance in history). The game ended in an exciting draw. Since then, this game usually attracts the biggest crowd for any home/away fixture.

Before the match, a special Anzac Day service is held at the MCG. This ceremony includes the recognition of Australian War Veterans as well as a Flag Ceremony, including the playing of the Last Post and Australian National Anthem.

My friend Andrew Miller, rates this game as 'noisier' than your typical Grand Final. *'A packed arena with loyalties about evenly split makes for an amazing atmosphere'.* The games themselves are hard fought (though the score lines aren't very close most years) as to be expected between two of the heavyweight teams of the competition with a rivalry dating back almost 130 years. In the modern-day ANZAC Day games Collingwood holds the edge having won 15 to Essendon's 9 with the one drawn game. James Hird

(Essendon) and Scott Pendlebury (Collingwood) have each won 3 Anzac Day medals for having been judged best on ground.

While the game has been a huge success for the AFL, some critics point out that the league has promoted the match to such an extent that it exploits the sacredness & solemnity of the Anzac story. Some of the other clubs feel the game should be shared around as previously happened. That debate will no doubt continue.

Since the 1990s there have been numerous Anzac Day games played in cities other than Melbourne, including Wellington, New Zealand. The Fremantle Dockers have been hosting an ANZAC game since 1996 - the club's Len Hall tribute game is either played on Anzac Day itself or over the weekend closest to Anzac Day.

Great Coaches

Three of the league's greatest coaches have coached Collingwood to premiership success, namely Jock McHale, Leigh Matthews and Mick Malthouse.

Jock McHale Coached 38 seasons, 714 games, 66% winning

average, 8 premierships in 16 Grand Finals - all with Collingwood. Legend status in Australian Football League Hall of Fame.

His name will forever be associated with his beloved Magpies. He played 261 games for Collingwood in the early 1900s and set the then league record of 191 consecutive games played between 1906-1917. He played in two premiership sides in 1910 and 1917 (the latter achieved while he was player coach). His remarkable longevity of 38 years coaching the team began in 1912 and between 1919-1936 he coached the Magpies to a further 7 Grand Final wins. McHale's total of 8 premierships as coach is still the league record. The Jock McHale Medal has been awarded to the winning Grand Final coach since the 2001 season. The medal was later retrospectively awarded to all the winning coaches between 1950-2000.

McHale was not at the ground on the day when the Magpies won their fourth straight flag in 1930 due to a bout of the flu. He is still given credit for that victory. In 1953 he helped Phonse Kyne and the Collingwood coaching staff plot the team's upset Grand Final victory over Geelong. After the win (which broke a 17-year premiership drought) he became extremely emotional. The next day he unfortunately suffered a heart attack and passed away a week later.

<u>Mick Malthouse</u> Coached 30 seasons (6 - Footscray, 10 - West Coast, 12 - Collingwood, 2.3 - Carlton), 3 premierships, most games coached 718

He joined Collingwood in 2000 after successful stints at Footscray and West Coast. The 'Pies made the finals in 8 of his 12 seasons, winning one premiership and finishing runners-up on three other occasions. Malthouse coached the greatest number of senior games in history and is the most successful finals' coach in history.

<u>Leigh Matthews</u> Coached 20 seasons (10 - Collingwood, 10 - Brisbane), 4 premierships (1 Collingwood, 3 Brisbane), inaugural legend of AFL Hall of Fame.

After replacing Bob Rose as coach early in the 1986 season, Matthews was the coach who in 1990, finally brought premiership success back to Collingwood. After 32 years during which time the club had appeared in 8 losing Grand Finals, the 'Colliwobbles' were put to rest.

Great Indigenous Player

Leon Davis

'Neon Leon' played most of his 12-year career with the Magpies as a small forward and later in his career in defence. He earned goal of the year honours in 2008 and gained All Australian selection in 2009 and 2011. In the 2010 drawn Grand Final versus St Kilda he kicked a vital goal in the final term but otherwise had a quiet game. He was dropped for the GF replay but still received a premiership medal.

Great Goal Kickers

Dick Lee (Collingwood 1906-22) **707 goals**

He played 17 seasons for Collingwood in the early 20th century. He was the first player to notch 700 majors and still holds the league record for being the leading goal kicker a total of 7 times. Lee was one of 136 players inducted into the

AFL Hall of Fame when it was first established in 1996.

Gordon Coventry (Collingwood 1920-37) **1299 goals**

He joined the Magpies as Dick Lee's career was winding down and quickly established himself as the league's outstanding goal kicker for most of the 1920s-30s. He led the league in goals a total of 6 times, was the first player to ever kick 100 or more in a season (124 in 1929), was the first to kick 9 goals in a Grand Final (1928) and was the first to play 300 games. His record of 1299 career goals stood for 62 years before Tony Lockett surpassed it in 1999. Coventry won 5 premierships with the Magpies.

Ron Todd (Collingwood 1935-39) **327 goals**

Todd had a spectacular, albeit short 5-year career with the Magpies. He won VFL goal kicking honours in 1938 & '39 when he booted 120 and 121 respectively. One of only 8 players to average better than 4 goals per game, he kicked 23 goals in the 1939 finals' series, a record which was not bettered for 50 years until Gary Ablett Sr kicked 27 in the

1989 finals. Todd was enticed to cross to Williamstown in time for the 1940 season at a time when the VFA had ended its player-transfer agreement with the VFL and was aggressively recruiting star players from the VFL.

Peter McKenna (Collingwood, Carlton 1965-75, 1977) **874 goals**

Playing all but the last 11 games of his VFL career with the Magpies, McKenna had a mop-top hairstyle, genial grin, ability to take big marks and follow them up with goals. He was our game's media star in the late 1960s/early '70s! He still holds the record for having scored at least one goal in 121 straight games. He won back to back Coleman Medals in 1972-73. In the 1970 Grand Final, McKenna had dominated in the first half kicking 5 of his 6 goals as the Maggies surged to a 44-point halftime lead. Unfortunately, late in the second quarter he collided heavily with team mate Des Tuddenham and was concussed. While he finished the game, he had little influence in the second half as Collingwood faded - but for his concussion the result of that game may have been different.

Collingwood-Geelong rivalry

Geelong's first VFL premiership win in 1925 was over Collingwood. Five years later the Magpies returned the favour by defeating the Cats in the GF, winning their league record 4th consecutive flag at the same time. A few years after that in 1937, the same two teams met in an enthralling Grand Final which Geelong won - thereby denying the Maggies a second 'threepeat'. In 1952 & '53 Geelong again met Collingwood in the GF, winning easily the first time but losing a close one in 1953. In Round 14 of the 1953 season it was the Magpies who finally ended Geelong's record 23 game winning streak (this record still stands today) with a 20-point win at Kardinia Park. Geelong's form dropped off after that. They lost 3 of their final 5 games, then were soundly beaten by Collingwood in the second-semi. Having worked out how to beat Geelong, the 'Pies went on with it and won the Grand Final by 2 goals over the Cats - thus denying Geelong *their* chance for a 'threepeat' of premierships.

In the modern era these two clubs have re-ignited their old rivalry. People remember that Geelong were the dominant team of season 2007 and that they steam-rolled Port Adelaide by a record 119 points in that year's Grand Final.

This was Geelong's first premiership victory since 1963 but the Cats very nearly didn't make it to the 'dance' that year, after they only narrowly defeated the 'Pies by 5 points in a tense preliminary final. The following season Geelong dropped only one game during the home-away rounds - you guessed it... to Collingwood by a massive 86 points! The two teams met in preliminary finals in both 2009 and 2010, with each team winning *en route* to a premiership. In 2011 the 'Pies and Cats contested a Grand Final for the first time in 58 years - thanks to a big last quarter Geelong won by 38 points. This was Geelong's third victory over Collingwood in season 2011 and interestingly, were the only games the Magpies lost all year.

Collingwood-Melbourne rivalry

This rivalry was particularly strong during the second half of the 1950s and up to 1964. These two teams met in 9 finals between 1955-64. In 1955, '56, '58, '60 and 1964, Melbourne won the Second-Semi to advance straight to the GF. Collingwood had the longer journey to get to the GF as by losing the Second-Semi (as they always did) to the Dees, the 'Pies had to then win the Preliminary Final to get another crack at Melbourne in the GF. While the Magpies did lose 4 of those 5 Grand Finals, the one time that they famously beat the Demons in 1958 was the one they particularly cherish. By defeating the Dees in the '58 Grand Final, Collingwood denied Melbourne the chance to equal the 'Pies' league record of 4 consecutive premierships (1927-1930). This is a record that no other team has equalled or surpassed in the last 90 years.

Worth mentioning also is that the 1958 Collingwood-Melbourne match at the MCG on the Queen's Birthday public holiday saw a record non-finals crowd of 99,256 witness this top of the table clash.

Victoria Park

Collingwood's famous home ground for over a century is located just 4kms from Melbourne's city centre. The park was established in 1879 in a spot formerly known as Dight's Paddock and three years later was given to 'the citizens of Collingwood for their resort and recreation'. A cricket pitch and cycling track were installed shortly afterwards.

Although Collingwood FC formed later (1892) and therefore joined the VFA later than the other top VFA teams, they quickly showed their credentials and by 1896 were crowned VFA premiers. Not only were they competitive right from the start, they garnered a huge support base almost immediately. In their very first game an estimated 16,000 spectators crammed in to Victoria Park to watch the game!

For the next 60 years, Collingwood FC had a series of short-term leases (usually 7 years) with the local City of Collingwood (now Yarra) council to use the ground. During this time the Ladies Stand (1900), Members Stand (1909) and Jack Ryder Stand (1929) were built. After the club won the 1953 premiership, they sought a longer-term lease which they eventually succeeded in getting. The proviso was that the club would need to make regular ground improvements. To this end in 1959 the Collingwood Social Club building was opened at the ground (now the Bob Rose Stand), the RT Rush Stand went up in 1966 and in 1969 the Sherrin Stand (which replaced the 60-year-old Members' Stand).

Victoria Park was Collingwood's 'fortress' for a very long time. It was a difficult place for visiting teams to win a game and opposition supporters didn't much like going there, knowing they would be vastly outnumbered by parochial

Magpie fans. Even before the Great Depression began there was a fair bit of unemployment in Collingwood. For many die-hard Magpie fans, seeing their team win at Victoria Park at least provided a highlight, especially during the tough years of the 1930s. Home games would always be packed with spectators – the attendance record of 47,000 fans was set in 1948 in a game between Collingwood-South Melbourne.

Moving home games away from Victoria Park: the team's gradual move away from its traditional home ground started in the late 1980s and coincided with the league's expansion towards a national competition. Football was growing in popularity and it made commercial sense for Collingwood to stage at least some of their home games at the bigger grounds, namely the MCG and VFL Park. Thousands more people could and did attend their games at those venues. This trend continued throughout the 1990s until finally the club played its final home game at Vic Park versus the Brisbane Lions in Round 22 of the 1999 season.

It was definitely the end of an era but it wasn't the end of Victoria Park, as the ground is protected under the Victorian Heritage Register. In recent years a number of renovations/upgrades have taken place. Collingwood's AFL Women's Team is based there and the club's VFL team plays a lot of their home games at the ground. While the senior AFL team no longer trains or plays at Victoria Park, many fans will always regard the venue as the club's spiritual home.

Collingwood's Team of the Century

B: *Harold Rumney, Jack Regan, Syd Coventry (Capt)*

HB: *Billy Picken, Albert Collier, Nathan Buckley*

C: *Thorold Merrett, Bob Rose, Darren Millane*

HF: *Des Fothergill, Murray Weideman, Dick Lee*

F: *Phonse Kyne, Gordon Coventry, Peter Daicos*

Foll: *Len Thompson, Des Tuddenham, Harry Collier*

Int: *Tony Shaw, Wayne Richardson, Marcus Whelan, Gavin Brown*

Coach *James "Jock" McHale*

Essendon Bombers

☆☆☆

♪♫ *"See the Bombers fly up, up...!"* ♪♫

Essendon - 'The 'Dons' or 'Bombers'

One of footy's best known teams was formed in 1872 by members of the Royal Agricultural Society, the Melbourne Hunt Club and the Victorian Wool Brokers. The team joined the VFA in 1878 and was very successful, winning 4 consecutive premierships (1891-94) shortly before it broke away as one of the founding-member clubs of the new VFL in 1896.

Home Grounds - East Melbourne Cricket Ground, Windy Hill, MCG & Docklands

For the first few years the club's home base was at Flemington Hill. In 1882 the club applied to the City of Essendon to play their home matches at the Essendon Cricket Ground. The application was turned down by the mayor who stated that the Essendon ground was "suitable only for the gentlemens' game of cricket"! Instead, the club ended up playing their home games at the East Melbourne Cricket Ground for the next 40 years (1882-1921). Back in the 1880s when spectators mainly walked to the ground on match days, this distant location didn't sit too well with many of their supporters. In 1921 the East Melbourne Cricket Ground was demolished to expand the Flinders Street rail yard and Essendon needed to find a new home.

Their first preference was to move to the North Melbourne Cricket Ground (Arden Street) as many of their players and supporters came from this area. The North Melbourne football club was all in favour as they saw such a move as a way for them to finally get into the VFL (many pundits predicted Essendon would have been taken over or rebranded had they been based there). The proposed relocation fell through when the VFA, who were desperate to retain their use of the North Melbourne ground, successfully appealed to the State Government to block the move. Four decades after being rejected to use the Essendon Cricket Ground, the club was welcomed back - not only that, the Council announced it would invest £12,000 on ground improvements.

Interestingly, the ground's nickname of 'Windy Hill' was only popularised from the mid-1950s by former Collingwood captain and by then sports' columnist Lou Richards - so named because of its windy reputation. Windy Hill also had the reputation of being a violent place for players, and was the site of several ugly incidents over the years. The most infamous of these was the "Battle of Windy Hill", when a brawl broke out between players, team officials, trainers, spectators and police at half-time during an Essendon-Richmond match in 1974.

A year later during the second quarter of the Essendon-Carlton game numerous players were involved in a brawl which saw 8 players face 11 charges at the tribunal. After a marathon tribunal sitting a total of 10 weeks of suspensions were handed out to the Blues' Ashman, Austin & Pennell, while the Bombers' Moloney & Close got a combined total of 4 weeks! (In addition to fighting, Carlton kicked a phenomenal score of 14.1 in this quarter on their way to an 80-point win!) Another memorable incident at the ground saw Hawthorn's Leigh Matthews break a behind post after running into it during play in a 1982 game!

The Bombers played 628 games at the venue in 70 seasons and had a 67% winning record - in 1992 after a poll of members, they moved their home games to the MCG, but retained Windy Hill as their training & administrative headquarters until 2013.

Nicknames - 'Same Olds', 'The Dons', 'Bombers'

The club's early nickname "The Same Old Essendon" came from the title and hook of a song performed by a band of supporters who regularly occupied a certain spot in the grandstand on match days. It was popular until just after World War I when it fell into disuse as did the other two occasionally used nicknames 'Sash Wearers' and 'Essendonians'. About the time the club moved back to the Essendon Cricket Ground, 'The Dons' (as in EssenDON) came into widespread use. The other very common nickname 'Bombers' started in 1940 at the beginning of World War II and was a reflection of the club's close proximity to Essendon Aerodrome.

Miscellany

Essendon is a team used to success and they have had plenty of that during their storied history. They have performed consistently to amass a record 16 premierships (a record they share with Carlton), although non-Essendon supporters will quickly point out that two of those flags came in the only two years when a Grand Final match was ***not*** actually played (in 1897 & 1924 a 'round-robin' format determined the premiership winner). Until 2020, the Bombers had **never** gone as long as 20 years between premierships - their previous longest drought was 19 seasons between 1965-1984.

Essendon were the dominant team of the 1940s, led by their great champion Dick Reynolds, who, as playing captain-coach, led them to 8 Grand Final appearances for 4 premierships between 1941-1950. Much later under the incredible 27-year coaching reign of Kevin Sheedy (1981-2007), the club won 4 more premierships and played in the finals many times. In season 2000, the Bombers were so dominant, they lost only one game (narrowly in Round 21 to the Western Bulldogs) for the entire year and won the Grand Final by 65 points. They also won the pre-season competition that season. It was an all-round team effort by Essendon in 2000 with some of their best players being James Hird, Matthew Lloyd, Steve Alessio, Mark Mercuri, Dustin Fletcher and Michael Long. In recent times the club has faced many challenges since their infamous 2013 supplements' scandal.

Additional Information supplied by friend John Coldham: *I thought that you might be interested to know that the Essendon Football Club was founded by my great, great grandfather Robert McCracken in 1872. As the founder he was also the first president. The club's first home ground was McCracken's Paddock which was part of Robert's Ascot Vale home.*

Robert's son and my grandmother's father, Alex, played for Essendon and was also later president. The McCrackens were very wealthy brewers - McCracken Breweries became Carlton & United Breweries in 1907.

ANZAC Day Games

Anzac Day has been a very important occasion for

over 100 years and from the 1920s to 1959, **no** VFL matches were conducted on 25th April. It took an Act of Parliament in 1960 to allow matches to be played on this solemn day. The first two games to be played on Anzac Day after the restrictions were lifted took place on Monday 25th April 1960 with Fitzroy playing Carlton at Brunswick Street and St Kilda playing Melbourne at the Junction Oval.

If ANZAC day fell on a weekday, between 2-3 matches were usually scheduled, with some of the gate receipts being handed over to the RSL. Over the years prior to 1995, there were several ANZAC Day games which attracted very large crowds - most notably the Carlton vs Essendon clash at VFL Park in 1975 (77,000+) and the Richmond vs Collingwood game at the MCG in 1977 (92,000+). The VFL even scheduled a double header on ANZAC Day in 1986 at the MCG. This experiment didn't work due to major logistical problems nor did it attract many spectators - a total of 'only' 40,000 fans for the two games between Melbourne-Sydney and North Melbourne-Geelong.

Sheedy has an idea: while pottering in his garden in 1994, then long-serving Essendon coach Kevin Sheedy started thinking, 'How could football honour those who served, including the legendary Anzacs of World War 1 in the best way possible?' At the time interest in and attendance at ANZAC Day activities was growing. Sheedy's vision was to have an annual game on ANZAC Day between Essendon & Collingwood. Officials from both clubs met and included RSL President Bruce Ruxton in their meeting. The concept was then worked through with the AFL and the following year the first ANZAC Day clash between these two giants of the league took place in front of a crowd of 94,825 (second largest home & away attendance in history). The game ended in an exciting draw. Since then this particular fixture has usually attracted the biggest crowd for any home & away game.

Before the match, a special Anzac Day service is held at the MCG. This ceremony includes the recognition of Australian War Veterans as well as a Flag Ceremony, including the playing of the Last Post and Australian National Anthem.

My friend Andrew Miller, rates this game as 'noisier' than your typical Grand Final. *'A packed arena with loyalties about evenly split makes for an amazing atmosphere'.* The games themselves are hard fought (though the score lines aren't very close most years) as to be expected between two of the heavyweight teams of the competition with a rivalry dating back almost 130 years. In the modern-day ANZAC Day games Collingwood holds the edge having won 15 to Essendon's 9 with the one drawn game. James Hird (Essendon) and Scott Pendlebury (Collingwood) have each won 3 Anzac Day medals for having been judged best on ground.

While the game has been a huge success for the AFL, some critics point out that the league has promoted the match to such an extent that it exploits the sacredness & solemnity of the Anzac story. Some of the other clubs feel the game should be shared around as previously happened. That debate will no doubt continue.

Since the 1990s there have been numerous Anzac Day games played in cities other than Melbourne, including Wellington, New Zealand. The Fremantle Dockers have been hosting an ANZAC game since 1996 - the club's Len Hall tribute game is either played on Anzac Day itself or over the weekend closest to Anzac Day.

Great Indigenous Footballers

The 2020 ***'Dreamtime at the 'G'*** match between Richmond-Essendon was played in Darwin due to the Covid-19 pandemic and its serious impact on Melbourne. This match is usually the major fixture during the league's annual Indigenous Round, now called the **Sir Doug Nicholls** Round, designed to recognize and celebrate indigenous players & culture. Essendon has had many terrific indigenous footballers over the years - a short profile of two of their best follows.

Gavin Wanganeen

He was born in Mount Gambier SA and had a distinguished career with the Port Adelaide Magpies in the SANFL, Essendon and Port Adelaide Power. Playing in various positions throughout his 300+ game career, he was a damaging on-baller, was sometimes used as a rebound defender and also could be a keen goal kicker. In 1993 he was a key member of Essendon's 'Baby Bombers' team which won the AFL premiership and he had the distinction of winning the Brownlow Medal that same season. He returned to South Australia in 1997 to become the inaugural captain of the newly formed Port Adelaide Power.

Michael Long

Selected at #23 in the 1988 national draft, Long played 190 games for Essendon between 1989-2001. He played mainly in the mid-field but unfortunately had long periods on the side lines due to recurring knee injuries. He missed the entire 1994 season due to a knee injury and between 1996-98 only managed 16 games due to injuries. Probably his career game was the 1993 AFL Grand Final when he gathered 33 possessions to help inspire the Bombers to a comfortable victory over Carlton. Long won the Norm Smith Medal that day and was thrilled to have the medal presented to him by fellow Tiwi Islander and 1982 Norm Smith Medallist, Maurice Rioli. Post-football Long has become a spokesperson for Indigenous Australians through the Michael Long Foundation which funds education and football programs for indigenous Australians.

Great Coaches

Dick Reynolds Coached 22 seasons, 66% winning average, 4 premierships as captain-coach of Essendon, inaugural legend in AFL Hall of Fame, AFL Team of the Century (half forward flank).

In addition to his glittering coaching record, Reynolds won 3 Brownlow Medals (1934, '37, '38) and held the record for games played (320) for the Bombers for almost 40 years (he still ranks in third spot behind Dustin Fletcher and Simon Madden). All of his premierships were achieved when he was the club's playing captain-coach in 1942, '46, '49 and 1950. Under Reynolds, Essendon dominated the late 1940s and but for some terrible kicking for goal in the 1947 & '48 Grand Finals, his team would have won 5 straight premierships. Dick Reynolds was inducted into the AFL Hall of Fame as a Legend when it first opened in 1996.

Did you know?

Dick Reynolds established a VFL record for the highest number of games played in 1951 - he appeared in only 1 game that season... his 320th game. The previous mark had been set by Richmond's playing captain-coach Jack Dyer who retired as a player in 1949 having played 312 games. I checked Reynolds' playing statistics and noted that he managed to get through a 19-year career with very few (serious) injuries - he averaged just under 17 games per year in an era when there were only 18 home & away matches. Reynolds' record of 320 games stood for almost 20 years until 1970 when Footscray's Ted Whitten established a new mark of 321.

Kevin Sheedy Coached 29 seasons (27 with Essendon, 2 with GWS), 4 premierships with Essendon, AFL Hall of Fame Legend, coach of Essendon's Team of the Century, holds the combined record of games played & coached at senior level - a phenomenal 929.

He ranks third in total games coached at 678 and led the Bombers to 4 premierships in his 27 years at the helm. As a coach he would not hesitate to move players to different positions in an effort to inspire his team. A famous example of this was the 1984 Grand Final when Sheeds made a number of positional changes at three quarter time, which resulted in the Bombers storming home in the final term to turn a 23-point deficit vs Hawthorn into a 24-point victory! He is also regarded as being one of the game's great thinkers.

Great Goal Kickers

John Coleman (Essendon 1949-54) **537 goals**

Despite his career being cut short by a knee injury after only 5.5 seasons, Coleman left an indelible mark on our game. Consider the following: he led the league in goals in 4 of his 5 full seasons; he scored 12 goals on debut in 1949 (including a goal with his first kick!) and kicked 100 for that season; while not overly tall (185 cm) he had this incredible ability to leap very high into the air from a standing start; he overcame a lot of hair tugging, head locks, thuggery & abuse generally by opposition players (and fans) who tried (usually in vain) to stop him. Long-time Essendon fans still loathe Carlton's Harry Caspar, who, on the eve of the 1951 finals provoked Coleman to such an extent that the star retaliated. Both men were suspended for 4 matches for striking but for Essendon, this meant that Coleman would be unavailable for the finals - they would go down to Geelong by only 11 points in the Grand Final.

During his 98-game career, Coleman was held goal-less on only one occasion - against Fitzroy at Brunswick Street in 1952. He made up for it in early 1954 by kicking his career-high of 14 goals in one game... against Fitzroy! Tragically in his very next game, he sustained the injury (dislocated knee including cartilage and ligament damage) which suddenly ended his amazing career at the age of 25 (he had two operations but despite several comeback attempts, never played again).

In May 2014, 60 years after Coleman played his final game, AFL medical commissioner Harry Unglik suggested that 'modern technology would likely have ensured a full recovery for the Essendon superstar's knee.' Surgical methods in the 1950s were archaic by modern-day standards and a similar injury today would require about a 6-week recovery period.

Just imagine if Coleman had been able to keep playing... Melbourne might not have been such a dominant force during the late 1950s and Gordon Coventry's phenomenal goal-kicking record might have been challenged well before Tony Lockett and Jason Dunstall arrived on the scene.

Coleman also proved to be an exceptional coach, guiding the Bombers to two flags (1962 & '65) during his 6 years as head coach.

Legacy: in 1981 the VFL decided to award a medal to its leading goal kicker for the home/away rounds, which is duly named the Coleman Medal.

Matthew Lloyd (Essendon 1995-2009) **926 goals**

Debuting at age 17 in the 1995 season, he had a distinguished career with the Bombers and is their all-time leading goal kicker. He was known for his strong over-head marking and his accurate left boot. On set shots from inside 50 he almost always converted and he also made quite a few from outside the arc. Lloyd won 3 Coleman medals in 2000, '01, '03 and was a member of Essendon's all-conquering premiership team in 2000. Lloyd is one of few players to register a goal with his first kick and in 2007 won 'Goal of the Year' honours for his back-heeled goal whilst surrounded by opposition players. He had a number of serious injuries over the years and decided to retire at the age of 31, shortly after the bump on Brad Sewell at the end of the 2009 season.

Essendon's Team of the Century

B: *Gavin Wanganeen, Fred Baring, Tom Fitzmaurice*

HB: *Barry Davis, Wally Buttsworth, Harold Lambert*

C: *Reg Burgess, Jack Clarke, Michael Long*

HF: *James Hird, Ken Fraser, Terry Daniher*

F: *Bill Hutchison, John Coleman, Albert Thurgood*

Foll: *Simon Madden, Tim Watson, Dick Reynolds (Capt)*

Int: *Mark Thompson, Keith Forbes, Frank Maher, Billy Griffith*

Coach *Kevin Sheedy*

Fremantle Dockers

☆☆☆

♪♫ "*Freo... Way To Go...*" ♪♫

The port city of Fremantle in Western Australia has a rich football history dating back to 1885 when the WAFL was founded. The area was so strong in Aussie Rules that *East Fremantle* and *South Fremantle* won 24 of the first 34 WAFL championships. When the AFL determined to have a second West Australian club, Fremantle was the logical location. The club joined as the competition's 16th team in 1995.

Nickname: club officials were in no doubt that the club's nickname needed to reflect the strength of the people of Fremantle as well as the area's close links to the port and the sea. Dolphins, Mariners, Stingrays, Seagulls, Sailors & Vikings were all considered but inaugural club chairman Ross Kelly favoured Dockers. There was a snag however due to the association some people might make with the former *Federated Ship Painters & Dockers Union,* which had been de-registered in 1993 after a criminal investigation! Some fancy footwork by Kelly and CEO David Hatt saw the name get over the line... the two claimed that the name was derived from the reliable afternoon sea breeze known as the 'Fremantle Doctor' which helped blow sailing ships in to the port of Fremantle. This story was apparently a white lie but it makes for good reading in *Wikipedia*!

Clearly the Dockers have had modest success over the years, especially compared to their cross-town rivals West Coast. It took 9 seasons for Freo to first play in the finals in 2003. They are still searching for their first flag, having made it to one Grand Final in 2013. They also won the minor premiership in 2015 and Nat Fyfe has won 2 Brownlow Medals in recent seasons. Probably the club's best-known player over many years is Matt Pavlich who played his entire career for Fremantle and was selected as an All-Australian player 6 times between 2002-2008. He is one of only 3 players to play 350+ games and kick 700+ goals (Kevin Bartlett and Bernie Quinlan being the other two).

When you consider their relative ladder positions, the Dockers often punch above their weight in the local derby versus West Coast. After losing their first 9 games against the Eagles, honours are virtually even between the two sides since 1999 (overall Freo has won 20 times to 31 for WCE). According to John Worsfold the main/only topic of conversation in Perth in the week leading up to a Western Derby is about the big game.

Fremantle's Len Hall ANZAC Day tribute game

Since the 1990s there have been numerous Anzac Day games played in cities other than Melbourne. The Fremantle Dockers have been hosting an ANZAC game since 1996 - the club's Len Hall tribute game is either played on Anzac Day itself or over the weekend closest to this sacred day. Hall played a critical role in three great battles during World War I.

1. He was a machine gunner at Gallipoli.
2. He rode in the Light Horse Brigade of the Desert Mounted Corps in the capture of Beersheba, Palestine, in 1917.
3. He rode with Colonel Thomas E Lawrence - known as Lawrence of Arabia - to liberate Damascus in 1918.

Hall was West Australia's last surviving Gallipoli veteran when he passed in early 1999 at the age of 101. Lest we forget.

Great Goal Kicker

Jeff Farmer (Melbourne, Fremantle)

Nick-named "The Wizard" for his uncanny ability to create goals out of nothing, Farmer played 7 seasons for both Melbourne and Freo. He played a total of 249 games and kicked 483 goals (224 of those with Freo). Farmer was one of our game's most exciting players to watch but also got himself in trouble both on and off the footy field.

Great Indigenous Player

Dale Kickett (Fremantle with short stints at Fitzroy, WCE, St Kilda, Essendon)

A strong defender whose quick dash out of defence could electrify the crowd, Kickett played a total of 181 games, most of them for Fremantle between 1995-2002. He was initially drafted by Fitzroy but never could get settled in the big city of Melbourne. When he was traded to the Eagles in time for the 1991 season, he only managed 2 games - the Eagles already had a really strong list and Kickett was subsequently de-listed. He finally found his niche at Freo starting in their inaugural year under his former Claremont coach, Gerard Neesham. He is related to Derek Kickett and Buddy Franklin.

Did you Know? A bit more information about Fremantle!

1. Ben Allan was the club's first captain in the 1995-96 seasons. He had been a premiership player with Hawthorn in 1991 and played with Claremont in the WAFL prior to that. Allan also helped the club as a caretaker coach in 2001

after Damian Drum was sacked.

2. Peter Mann holds the record for most goals in a game for the club with 10 majors.

3. Peter Bell is the only Dockers' player so far to make it to the AFL Hall of Fame. He was a dual premiership player with North Melbourne before crossing to Freo in 2001 where he had a very successful 7.5 seasons.

4. The Doig Medal is awarded to Fremantle's 'Best & Fairest' each year. The award is named after the legendary Fremantle football family the Doigs. The family had a total of 17 family members play for either East Fremantle or South Fremantle in the WAFL.

5. The club's mascot since 2003 has been Johnny 'The Doc' Docker, a surfie.

Fremantle's Silver Anniversary Team (1995-2019)

B: *Roger Hayden, Shane Parker, Antoni Grover*

HB: *Michael Johnson, Luke McPharlin, Dale Kickett*

C: *Stephen Hill, David Mundy, Shaun McManus*

HF: *Michael Walters, Matt Pavlich, Clive Waterhouse*

F: *Jeff Farmer, Tony Modra, Hayden Ballantyne*

Foll: *Aaron Sandilands, Nat Fyfe, Peter Bell*

Int: *Paul Hasleby, Lachie Neale, Troy Cook, Michael Barlow, Ryan Crowley, Justin Longmuir, Ben Allan*

Geelong Cats

♪♩♪ *"We are Geelong, the greatest team of all..."* ♪♩♪

The Geelong Football Club is the second oldest Aussie Rules football club (after Melbourne), founded in 1859. They were one of the inaugural teams when the VFA started in 1877 and were one of the 8 breakaway teams to form the VFL in 1896. It is interesting to note that in the late 1890s, both Ballarat and Bendigo were larger regional cities than Geelong. However, Geelong had been playing in the 'Metropolitan' section of the VFA since 1879 and had won 7 VFA premierships - the most of any club. They were therefore certainties to be part of the breakaway VFL. In the new league however, premiership success was a long time coming and it took until 1925 before Geelong won its first VFL flag.

How the club got its nickname

Two very early nicknames for the club were 'Seagulls' and 'Pivotonians' – the latter because Geelong was regarded as a pivotal point for shipping and rail in Victoria. In 1923 the term Cats was used for the first time. A run of losses that season prompted a local cartoonist to suggest that the club needed a black cat to bring it good luck! The name stuck, especially since Geelong won their first premiership soon afterwards.

Famous player/what's in a name?

Edward 'Carji' Greeves was a brilliant midfielder for Geelong from 1923-'33 and helped the club win their first two flags. He also had the distinction of winning the inaugural Brownlow Medal in 1924, the highest individual award in the league. Greeves is a member of Geelong's team of the century and was duly elected to the AFL Hall of Fame when it first opened in 1996. His nickname 'Carji' was bestowed when he was an infant and is based on a character of the same name in *'A Country Girl'*, a popular musical of the day. Another interesting titbit... Greeves' grandmother was briefly engaged to Tom Wills the famous cricketer ***and*** founder of Australian rules football. Finally, the 'Carji' Greeves medal is awarded to Geelong's best & fairest player each year.

Rivalries

In the modern era Geelong's keenest rivalry has been with Hawthorn. In the more distant past from the mid-1920s to the mid-1950s the Cats had a fierce rivalry with the Magpies and that rivalry is also pretty keen today as both teams have met in the finals a number of times this century.

Geelong-Collingwood

Geelong's first VFL premiership win in 1925 was over Collingwood. Five years later the Magpies returned the favour by defeating the Cats in the GF, winning their league record 4th consecutive flag at the same time. A few years after that in 1937, the same two teams met in an enthralling Grand Final which Geelong won - thereby denying the Maggies a second 'threepeat'. In 1952 & '53 Geelong again met Collingwood in the GF, winning easily the first time but losing a close one in 1953. In Round 14 of the 1953 season it was the Magpies who finally ended Geelong's record 23 game winning streak (this record still stands today) with a 20-point win at Kardinia Park. Geelong's form dropped off after that. They lost 3 of their final 5 games, then were soundly beaten by Collingwood in the second-semi. Having worked out how to beat Geelong, the 'Pies went on with it and won the Grand Final by 2 goals over the Cats - thus denying Geelong *their* chance for a 'threepeat' of premierships.

In the modern era these two clubs have re-ignited their old rivalry. People remember that Geelong were the dominant team of season 2007 and that they steam-rolled Port Adelaide by a record 119 points in that year's Grand Final. This was Geelong's first premiership victory since 1963 but the Cats very nearly didn't make it to the 'dance' that year, after they only narrowly defeated the 'Pies by 5 points in a tense preliminary final. The following season Geelong dropped only one game during the home-away rounds - you guessed it... to Collingwood by a massive 86 points! The two teams met in preliminary finals in both 2009 and 2010, with each team winning *en route* to a premiership. In 2011 the 'Pies and Cats contested a Grand Final for the first time in 58 years - thanks to a big last quarter Geelong won by 38 points. This was Geelong's third victory over Collingwood in season 2011 and interestingly those were the only games that the Magpies lost all year.

Geelong vs Hawthorn

For the last decade, the Easter round of footy has culminated with the Easter Monday match between Geelong & Hawthorn. Geelong beat the Hawks in the 1963 Grand Final but their rivalry only started to get intense from the mid-1980s. At Princes Park in 1985 Hawthorn's Leigh Matthews struck Geelong's Neville Bruns so hard that the latter broke his jaw. It was a particularly spiteful match with numerous reports. The umpires (who by the last quarter were struggling to control the game) missed the Bruns incident as it happened off the ball. In extraordinary circumstances the police were later called to investigate and Matthews was de-registered as a player for a month and found guilty of assault in the Magistrates' Court. The unfortunate incident soured the end of his stellar playing career.

1989 Grand Final: Hawthorn 21.18.144 defeated Geelong 21.12.138

During the strange days of isolation in 2020, many footy fans took to watching some of the great matches from years gone by. The 1989 Grand Final between Geelong and Hawthorn was a classic! It was memorable for many reasons... Hawthorn equalled Melbourne's league record (set between 1954-60) by appearing in their 7th straight GF, it was the second highest scoring GF ever played and it featured an exciting last quarter comeback by the Cats which almost snared them their first premiership in 26 years. The 282 points scored on the day were second only to the 327 recorded in the 1972 GF between Carlton-Richmond. Gary Ablett kicked 9 goals in a losing cause. It was also the last VFL Grand Final played before the league changed its name to the AFL in 1990.

Even more than the high scoring, what really sticks in the memory of many fans is how violent this contest was. Geelong's Mark Yeates deliberately charged Dermott Brereton a moment after the ball was bounced to start the game leaving Dermie with broken ribs and in excruciating pain. Brereton refused to come off the ground despite the injury, kicked 3 goals for the game and inspired his team's win. Geelong was definitely 'playing the man' in an effort to unsettle the more skilful Hawks. Hawthorn's Robert DiPierdomenico, John Platten, Gary Ayres and Darren Pritchard also got very heavily crunched and by game's end they had only 13 fit players on the ground. Still, it was back-to-back wins for the Hawks who confirmed their status as the dominant team of the 1980s (ahead of Carlton & Essendon).

Jump ahead 19 seasons and it was the Cats who entered the 2008 Grand Final as warm favourites to beat the Hawks. It wasn't to be however as wayward kicking in front of goal denied Geelong the chance to defend their premiership from the year before. The Cats loss was only their second defeat all year - very painful for their supporters.

Since the 2008 GF, the rivalry between Geelong-Hawthorn has grown in intensity and importance. Badly stung from losing the most important game of the year in 2008, Geelong won their next 11 games over Hawthorn, many of them by less than a kick. Almost all matches between these sides since 2007 have been played at the MCG, befitting of two teams that have dominated our competition for long periods over the last 14 years (between them, these two teams have won 7 of the last 14 flags). The Easter Monday clash is one of the most anticipated games of the year.

Miscellany. Geelong have had plenty of champion players over the years including, in more recent times, Doug Wade, Greg Williams, Gary Ablett Sr, Joel Selwood and Tom Hawkins. Their Brownlow Medallists in addition to Carji Greeves include Bernie Smith, Alistair Lord, Paul Couch, Jimmy Bartel, Gary Ablett Jr and Patrick Dangerfield. They continue to have a strong list, are a very well-managed club and are invariably near the top - finishing runners up in season 2020.

The Cats have won 9 VFL/AFL premierships but a few seasons ago applied to the AFL to request that their 7 VFA premierships be recognized by the AFL in their club's overall total. In 2016 this request was rejected by the AFL Commission - allowing such a request to go ahead would have required a complete overhaul of premiership tables involving all the other foundation VFL teams and some former VFA teams now playing in the AFL. Geelong hold the record for the highest score ever achieved in a match - their total of 37.17.239 versus the Brisbane Bears at Carrara Stadium (now Metricon Stadium) has stood the test of time since 1992. During World War II, Geelong was the only team forced to 'sit out' seasons 1942 and '43 - this wasn't because they had a much larger number of men called up to the army than other clubs, rather it was mainly due to travel restrictions at the time. *

**The Second World War had many effects on the organisation of football in Australia - below are some interesting snippets which I thought were worth sharing.*

- *For Geelong players who didn't go to war, temporary transfers to other clubs were available (with a limit of three per club).*

- *Both Melbourne and Collingwood struggled to field a team, and at one stage considered amalgamating into a joint team. Ultimately, they were both able to compete.*

- *Hawthorn and Collingwood withdrew their teams from the Reserves competition.*

- *Available servicemen were often called upon to make up the numbers - this accounts for the drop in form of the Melbourne team, who had won the previous three premierships.*

- *The VFA went into recess for three years between 1942-1944 during which time any of their eligible players were given temporary league permits.*

- *The Brownlow Medal was suspended until 1946.*

- *Many ground changes were also forced upon teams, as their usual home grounds were used in the war effort. The alternative grounds used were Yarraville Oval (Footscray), Toorak Park (St Kilda), Punt Road Oval (Melbourne) and Princes Park (South Melbourne).*

- *Government regulations meant the traditional matches held on the King's Birthday public holiday could not be played again until 1946.*

The Brownlow Medal

The Charles Brownlow medal has been awarded since 1924 to the player adjudged to be the 'fairest & best' in the league. It is the highest individual award in the competition and sometimes is informally referred to as "Charlie". The award was created and named in honour of Charles Brownlow a former Geelong player (1880-1891) and club secretary (1885-1923). Brownlow also served as VFL president in 1918-1919.

The current voting system involves the 3 field umpires conferring at the end of each game to determine the three 'fairest & best' players on the ground that day. They award 3 points for the best, 2 for second best and 1 for third best. This has been the voting system used for most years since the award's inception. Interestingly the VFL was the last of the 4 major competitions in the mainland states to introduce an award for its fairest & best player - the SANFL's Magarey Medal was first awarded in 1898, the WAFL's Sandover Medal in 1921 and the VFA's Woodham Cup in 1923.

Starting in 1981, if two or more players tally the highest number of votes, both/all receive a medal. Prior to 1981 had there been a tie, a countback system was used to determine one winner - the player who had the highest number of first place votes would win and if there was still a tie, the player with the highest number of second place votes would win.

In 1989 the league decided to retrospectively award

Brownlow Medals to the 8 players who had tied on votes but lost on a countback before 1981. Those 8 players were: Harry Collier (Collingwood) & Allan Hopkins (Footscray) 1930; Herbie Matthews (South Melbourne) & Des Fothergill (Collingwood) 1940; Col Austen (Hawthorn) 1949; Bill Hutchison (Essendon) 1952; Verdun Howell (St Kilda) 1959; Noel Teasdale (North Melbourne) 1965. **Note**: in 1940, Fothergill and Matthews could *not* be separated on countback, which prompted the league to keep the original medal and instead issue two replica medals!

The Brownlow Medal ceremony is held in the week preceding the Grand Final. The evening is a gala affair held at Crown Casino in Melbourne (a virtual event was conducted in 2020). Players and especially their partners have placed a major emphasis on fashion when attending the event, which has added another aspect to the evening in recent years. The Brownlow Medal count has been shown on TV since 1970.

Great Coaches

<u>Reg Hickey</u> Coached 17 seasons, 60% winning average, 3 premierships all with Geelong

Hickey joined the Cats in 1926 and was known for his

dashing runs out of defence. He was captain coach of the team for much of the 1930s, a decade in which Geelong won 2 flags. In the 1937 Grand Final, the score was tied at three quarter time between Geelong-Collingwood. In an effort to break the deadlock Hickey made a number of positional changes for the final quarter - something which was unheard of at the time. The changes worked as the Cats kicked away in the last quarter to win by 32 points. Hickey retired as a player in early 1940 but returned as coach for the period 1949-59. In the early 1950s, Geelong were the league's top team winning back to back premierships in 1951-52 and setting a record of 23 straight victories during 1952-53 which still stands!

<u>Chris Scott</u> Current coach of Geelong since 2011, 70% winning average, 1 premiership

Scott had a very successful playing career (215 games) with the Brisbane Bears/Lions and played in 2 premierships in 2001-02. He was appointed coach of Geelong at the end of the 2010 season. In his inaugural 2011 season the Cats won their first 13 games and went on to beat Collingwood in the Grand Final. It was a stunning start to Scott's coaching career

- he is the most recent first year coach to win a flag and at age 35 was the youngest coach to win a premiership since Alex Jesaulenko in 1979. Scott has amassed a phenomenal 70% winning record with the Cats in 10 seasons, but also has his critics who feel Geelong has had the personnel to win multiple premierships in the last decade.

Great Goal Kickers

Doug Wade (Geelong, North Melbourne 1961-75) **1057 goals**

He initially tried out for Melbourne in 1960, but ended up joining Geelong the following season instead. A prolific goal kicker he became only the second player (after Coventry) to score 1000 goals or more in his career and still ranks fourth on the all-time list. He won 4 Coleman Medals 3 for the Cats, 1 for North) and played in 2 premierships (one for each team).

Gary Ablett Sr. (Hawthorn & Geelong, 1982, 1984-96) **1031 goals**

Nicknamed "God" for his freakish, all-round skills and ability to kick goals, Ablett joined Hawthorn in 1982 when he played 6 games but never adjusted to big-city life. Ablett returned to country life the following year and then joined Geelong (for a $60,000 transfer fee) in 1984 for what turned out to be a very memorable 13-year career. Ablett played the majority of his career as a half-forward and when he turned it on, as he did during the 1989 finals' series, he was truly exhilarating to watch (he notched a record 27 goals in 4 finals' matches that season including a record-equalling 9 in the GF). Geelong coach Malcolm Blight put him at full forward starting in 1993. It was a move he relished and he won the Coleman Medal for three straight years between 1993-95, but the elusive premiership remained just that. A complex individual, Ablett became a born-again Christian in 1986 and wasn't particularly comfortable with the 'God' nickname bestowed upon him. He had numerous trips to the tribunal resulting in a number of suspensions. He retired in early 1991 but was talked into returning part way through the year.

Great Indigenous Player

Graham 'Polly' Farmer

Few players can be identified as having "revolutionized" the way a particular position is played. Graham 'Polly' Farmer was one of those rare players. He was the outstanding ruckman of his generation with his attacking tap outs and he was also brilliant in his use of long handballs. It was said that until Farmer came along, handball was usually considered a 'last resort option' but he showed how it could become a 'dangerous offensive weapon'. Farmer was born in Fremantle and joined East Perth as an 18-year old in 1953. During the next 9 years the club won 3 WANFL premierships, while Farmer won 7 club best & fairest awards and 3 Sandover medals. He crossed to Geelong in 1962 but unfortunately was injured in the very first game and missed the rest of the season. In 1963 Farmer was instrumental in leading the Cats to the VFL premiership - this was Geelong's last flag for 44 years! He finished equal second in the Brownlow medal count that season and won the club's best & fairest in both 1963 and '64. Returning to Perth in 1968 he became player-coach for West Perth and in his four seasons won a further two premierships. After his playing days were over, he also coached both Geelong and East Perth during the 1970s. Farmer has been awarded Legend Status in the Australian Football Hall of Fame.

Geelong's Team of the Century

B: *Bernie Smith, George Todd, John Newman*

HB: *Dick Grigg, Reg Hickey (Capt), Joe Slater*

C: *Michael Turner, Edward Greeves, Leo Turner*

HF: *Gary Ablett Sr, Fred Flanagan, Bob Davis*

F: *Henry Young, Doug Wade, Peter Pianto*

Foll: *Polly Farmer, Garry Hocking, Bill Goggin*

Int: *David Clarke, Paul Couch, Alec Eason, Les Hardiman*

Coach *Reg Hickey*

☆

Gold Coast Suns

♪♪ "*We are the Suns of the Gold Coast sky...*" ♪♪

The club took its place as the league's 17th team in 2011. It is based in the Gold Coast suburb of Carrara and plays its home games at Carrara (Metricon) Stadium. In 2009 when the licence was issued to bring a second Queensland team into the competition, one of the important considerations involved the redevelopment of Carrara Stadium. The stadium had previously been the home ground for the Brisbane Bears for their first few seasons in the league starting in 1987 but was in need of an upgrade. Fortunately, negotiations between the AFL and Queensland government were fruitful, with the AFL providing a small portion of the funding for the upgrade.

Gold Coast signed Gary Ablett Jr from Geelong to a multi-year contract in late 2010 and he was captain of the team for its first 6 seasons. While playing for the Suns, Ablett won his second Brownlow medal in 2013 to become only the fifth player in history to win Brownlow Medals with two different clubs (the others being Ian Stewart, Peter Moore, Greg Williams and Chris Judd). In 2017 he requested a trade back to his original club, Geelong.

Karmichael Hunt - the rugby experiment

The Suns also signed high-profile rugby league player Karmichael Hunt to join their fledgling team for the start of the 2011 season. The deal was partly subsidised by the AFL and involved Hunt having to do a fair bit of promotional & development work. Hunt's on-field performances were regarded as a bit of a mixed bag and due to injury problems in his last two years, he only managed 44 games in 4 seasons. One of his biggest highlights was kicking the winning goal, after the siren, in a game versus Richmond in 2012 - the goal helped Gold Coast break a lengthy winless drought. After leaving the Suns, Hunt returned to play Super Rugby for the Queensland Reds and NSW Waratahs. An exceptional athlete, he has represented Australia in both rugby league and rugby union and was the first player to play at senior level in both the AFL and the NRL. A year later another talented rugby player, Israel Folau, debuted for GWS - but also switched back to rugby after only 2 seasons. It is clearly very difficult to switch codes and make a similar impact in the new code at such a high level.

Promoting the game in Queensland and the NT

The Suns have done a lot to help promote the sport in Queensland and there is strong growth in junior football, Auskick programmes and the women's game. As is the case with all AFL teams the Suns contribute significantly to their local community. According to the club's website... 'in the last nine years the club and players have committed to more than 45,000 community volunteering hours with a strong focus on key social projects tackling domestic violence, youth homelessness and regional needs. This, combined with the development of Metricon Stadium and an average contribution to the local economy of some $38 million per year, means that the Suns are not only part of the future of Australian football but also an integral part of the Gold Coast's story'.

The club plays the occasional home game in Cairns, Townsville and Darwin. They have also played matches against Port Adelaide in Shanghai, China in 2017 and 2018 - these were the first matches to ever be played in China which counted for premiership points.

The Q Clash

The club's main rivalry is with the Brisbane Lions and their matches are commonly referred to as the Q Clash. The Suns won the first Q Clash back in 2011 by 8 points in a game played at The Gabba in Brisbane. It was the Suns' second-ever win in the AFL. Brisbane have since built a 13-6 lead over Gold Coast in the Q Clash through the 2020 season. Footy fans in the southern states may not be as familiar with this rivalry as they are with certain other league rivalries, but it is a strong one. During the 16th Q Clash in 2018 there were several feisty exchanges between the Suns' Touk Miller and Brisbane's Dayne Zorko. After the game Miller was quoted as saying 'we don't like each other' in reference to the rivalry between the two clubs - pretty much what you would expect in a strong, local rivalry.

The Marcus Ashcroft Medal is awarded to the player judged to be best on ground during the Q Clash matches. Gold Coast players who have won this medal include Gary Ablett Jr (twice), Touk Miller (twice), Jared Brennan, Charlie Dixon and Tom Lynch.

Marcus Ashcroft moved to the Gold Coast from Melbourne with his family at the age of 3. He played his junior football with the Southport Sharks before being drafted by the Brisbane Bears in time for the 1988 season. He played over 300 games for the Brisbane Bears/Lions and fittingly went out a winner after the 2003 season with his third straight premiership medal.

After his playing career finished Ashcroft continued to serve the game. He became part of the coaching panel with the second Queensland team, the Gold Coast Suns. where he served as their football manager from 2009 until the end of the 2017 season.

The future

Since 2018 the club has taken major steps forward under coach Stuart Dew. Club management have shown their faith in Dew by extending his contract for another 2 years through until the end of season 2022. The team got off to a strong start in 2020, winning three of their first four games before falling back. They have some good young players like Jack Likosius, Jack Bowes and teenage star Matt Rowell. Rowell put in some eye-catching performances in the first four rounds of the 2020 season before suffering a shoulder injury in the Round 5 clash versus Geelong - unfortunately the injury sidelined him for the remainder of the season. I expect that the Suns will play in their first finals' series in the next couple of years.

Gold Coast's Team of the Decade (2010-2019)

B: *Michael Rischitelli, Rory Thompson, Kade Kolodjashnij*

HB: *Adam Saad, Steven May, Jarrod Harbrow*

C: *Aaron Hall, David Swallow, Brayden Fiorini*

HF: *Jack Martin, Tom Lynch, Harley Bennell*

F: *Brandon Matera, Charlie Dixon, Alex Sexton*

Foll: *Jarrod Witts, Gary Ablett Jr, Dion Prestia*

Int: *Jared Brennan, Touk Miller, Peter Wright, Sam Day*

Greater Western Sydney Giants

♪♫ "*Well there's a big big sound...*
From the West of the town..." ♪♫

The Giants are the AFL's newest team, having joined as the 18th team in 2012. Thanks to very generous draft concessions and financial assistance from the AFL it didn't take long for GWS to become one of the better teams in the competition - they made the finals for 4 straight years from 2016 and played in their first Grand Final in 2019. They have helped grow the game in western Sydney as well as in Canberra (the team plays some games at Manuka Oval in the ACT).

The club's initial coach during seasons 2012 and 2013 was the legendary Kevin Sheedy. While he won only 3 games in those two seasons, he did much to set the team up for its more recent success. Let's look at some of their success.

After finishing last in their first two seasons, GWS started to steadily and then rapidly improve under the coaching of Leon Cameron. Climbing to 16th and then 11th in their third and fourth seasons, the Giants took a big step forward in 2016 by finishing 4th after the minor rounds. In their first ever finals' match the Giants defeated their cross-town rivals the Sydney Swans by 6 goals in a Qualifying Final - given that the Swans were minor premiers that season and were highly experienced in playing finals, this was no mean feat. The Giants weren't quite able to continue their run, losing a close Preliminary Final to the Western Bulldogs by 1 goal. Had they won that game the 2016 Grand Final would have been an all-Sydney affair!

The Giants went on to make the finals for the next 3 seasons and they won at least one finals' match in each of those years. Their best result was qualifying for the Grand Final against Richmond in 2019, defeating the Bulldogs in an elimination final, Brisbane in a semi-final and memorably just holding on in the Preliminary Final to beat a fast-finishing Collingwood by 4 points at the MCG. Unfortunately, they were out of their depth in their first Grand Final and after a tight first quarter went down to Richmond by 89 points. Still, it was an impressive feat for a brand new club to reach the GF in only its eighth season in the league.

In the Covid-19 2020 season, GWS suffered a drop in form and missed the finals for the first time since 2015. They just didn't seem to click, but they still have a strong list with players like Jeremy Finlayson, Lachie Whitfield, Toby Greene, Callan Ward & Phil Davis. Provided they don't lose too many of these players, I expect they will come back strongly next season.

Rivalries

GWS vs Western Bulldogs

These two teams have a way of really niggling each other and their matches can sometimes be very heated! They have played some very important games in recent years. In addition to the two matches mentioned above, their Round 22 clash in 2019 at Giants' Stadium was a critical game if the Bulldogs were going to make the finals that season. Against the odds and predictions of almost everyone, the Doggies rose to the occasion to stun the Giants, winning by 61 points. The win catapulted the Bulldogs into the top 8 for the first time since Round 3 and they maintained their spot in the season's final round. However, the Giants learned from their mistakes in that game to extract their revenge just a fortnight later. The Giants' 58-point win in the Elimination Final at Giants' Stadium reflected a 119-point turnaround from a fortnight earlier - footy can sometimes be quite unpredictable!

GWS vs Sydney Swans

Matches between the two sides are usually referred to as 'The Sydney Derby' and sometimes as 'The Battle of the Bridge'. The teams have played one another 19 times through to the end of 2020 with the Giants having won 7 of those games. Importantly from a GWS standpoint, they have won both times when the teams met in the finals, a 2016 Qualifying Final and 2018 Elimination Final.

The football pie in the Harbour City

Competing for a large slice of the football 'pie' in Sydney is not easy as NSW is still primarily a rugby state. I asked my friend Derek Hanna who grew up in Sydney's west for his thoughts about a developing rivalry between GWS and the Sydney Swans. Derek made some interesting observations which I share with you below.

GWS is still the "little brother" of the AFL in Sydney. I don't see it as a rivalry, more of a preference, as we support both teams until they play each other.

Sydney is fragmented, a real melting pot these days of Rugby League and Union, AFL, soccer etc.

In Melbourne you are expected to have an AFL team but in Sydney the answer to the question, 'Did you watch the footy,' is to say, 'What do you mean by footy'?

The above said, most Swans' supporters stuck with the Swans. I changed as soon as GWS came along because the games are easier to get to, our son had played in the local junior team (Baulkham Hills

Falcons) and I am a "Western Sydney Boy."

I was really interested to see how 2020 would go, given GWS's 1st Grand final appearance a year earlier and to see if a bunch of new supporters would get on board. It ended up being a disappointing season.

One interesting anecdote is that GWS has the same colours as the "State Rail Authority", so every train employee supports GWS. This can cause some confusion at a train station when the crowd arrives and leaves, particularly if you want to find a rail employee to ask a question. I have even heard announcements at a train station trying to help people know who is who!

In the initial couple of years GWS recruited Israel Folau from Rugby League. He had been a champion in that footy code but he never transferred across to the AFL game and eventually skipped codes again and went to Rugby Union. For me this was a big waste of time and money - yes, he is a good athlete but he was never going to be a champion on the AFL park.

Gold Coast and GWS took very different approaches to establishing a new AFL team. Gold Coast decided to get some experience straight away by obtaining players like Gary Ablett Jr. GWS decided to start with a very young, inexperienced team and build up over a number of years. This approach resulted in many losses and some wooden spoons to start with, but when the players developed, they all came good at the same time and playing in finals was the result. Kevin Sheedy did a good job. The GWS "Best and fairest" award is called the Kevin Sheedy Medal.

GWS Team of the Decade (2010-2019)

B: *Nick Haynes, Phil Davis, Heath Shaw*

HB: *Zac Williams, Adam Tomlinson, Lachie Whitfield*

C: *Josh Kelly, Callan Ward, Dylan Shiel*

HF: *Devon Smith, Jeremy Cameron, Tim Taranto*

F: *Toby Greene, Jonathon Patton, Steve Johnson*

Foll: *Shane Mumford, Stephen Coniglio, Adam Treloar*

Int: *Rory Lobb, Tom Scully, Jacob Hopper, Ryan Griffen*

Hawthorn Hawks

♪♪ "*We're a happy team at Hawthorn...*" ♪♪

Those who follow footy closely will likely know that Hawthorn are easily the most successful club of the last 60 years. They have amassed 13 premierships since 1961, winning at least one premiership in each decade and averaging a GF victory every 4.7 years! They have ***appeared*** in 19 Grand Finals during these 60 years and to put this in perspective, consider that only 4 other teams have even reached double figures in terms of GF appearances over the same period - Carlton & Collingwood with 13 appearances and Richmond & Essendon with 10, lag a long way behind the Hawks! The club has had much to celebrate over the last few decades - no wonder they are such a happy team!

I was curious to find out how the Hawks came to be so consistently good but looking at the early years of their history found that they were in fact the league's easy beats.

Foundation: between 1873-1898 there were at least 3 versions of clubs calling themselves Hawthorn Football Club which formed and disbanded after a fairly short time. These teams never played at VFA level. In 1902 the club was founded which would become the great team of today. Several district clubs merged that year to compete in the Metro Junior Football Association. In 1906 when Glenferrie Oval first opened the club merged with another successful junior club, the Hawthorn Rovers to become the Hawthorn City FC. In 1914 the club successfully applied to join the VFA and the word 'City' was dropped from the club's name. That same year the club adopted the colours gold & brown.

Nickname: the club's nickname in the early days was 'Maybloooms', although this name wasn't used too often. Maybllooms was likely adopted because the Hawthorn bush was also known as the May bush or May tree - both its flowers and the plant itself were referred to as 'Mayblooms'. The name 'Hawks' was adopted in 1943 at the time the legendary Roy Cazaly was coaching the club - the name apparently was suggested by Cazaly's daughter!

Hawthorn played 8 unremarkable seasons in the VFA before being one of the 3 clubs granted admission to the VFL in 1925. During their short stint in the VFA, the league went into recess in 1916-17 due to World War I and Hawthorn did not resume playing until 1919. The club only played in the finals once in the early 1920s. They certainly were not accepted to join the VFL in 1925 because they were a strong club - it may have been because admitting Hawthorn wasn't going to badly upset the metro recruiting zones of existing clubs and also that Hawthorn was not a 'rough area'?

Whatever the reasons, Hawthorn, Footscray and North Melbourne were given the nod to join the VFL in 1925 ahead of applications from Brighton, Caulfield, Prahran and Brunswick. Of the three new teams, Hawthorn were the underachievers. It took until 1957 before they finally qualified for the finals - during those 33 years they collected 10 wooden spoons, had 2 winless seasons and were the league's perennial whipping boys. Their location was remote from major industrial areas and consequently the club was devoid of business or political patrons available to clubs like Carlton, Collingwood & Richmond. At times they appeared to have a casual attitude to playing footy and during the tough years of the 1930s, could not always afford to pay their players.

Gradual turnaround: the year 1950 saw the arrival of John Kennedy Sr at the club as a player, but in that same season off-field troubles saw the team's two best players (Col Austen & Alec Albiston) leave and the team failed to win a single game! Two years later their fortunes started to improve when Jack Hale took over as coach and the club also benefitted from "receiving dividends from the VFL's finals revenue, which helped make them more competitive financially." In the mid-1950s they recruited players John Peck, Graham Arthur and Brendan Edwards - all of whom were instrumental in finally leading the team out of the wilderness. Arthur captained Hawthorn to its first flag in 1961 and Edwards was acknowledged to be best on ground in the Grand Final. Kennedy took over as coach in 1960 and proved to be a master motivator & tactician. The club had one other GF appearance in the 1960s but otherwise missed the finals for the rest of the decade. Kennedy wasn't in charge the entire time as he accepted a teaching position in Hamilton for 3 years. Hawthorn was one of the teams to most benefit from the country zoning that was introduced in 1968 - gaining the footy-rich Mornington Peninsula area.

The team really started to fire from 1971 onwards. Peter Crimmins, Don Scott, Peter Hudson, Peter Knights and Leigh Matthews had all joined the Hawks in the late 1960s and soon became stars. Hawthorn won 3 flags in the 1970s and had a particularly keen rivalry with North Melbourne, playing them in the GF 3 times in 4 years (for 2 wins) and losing to them in the 1977 preliminary final. After Kennedy retired, former captain David Parkin coached the team to a premiership in his second season in 1978. In 1981 after Parkin moved to Carlton, Allan Jeans was appointed coach. A proven coach inheriting a highly talented team like Hawthorn made the Hawks even more formidable. Between 1983-91 the Hawks played in the Grand Final 8 out of 9 years, winning five premierships. Their keenest rivalries were with

Essendon and Carlton during the 1980s. Dermott Brereton, Jason Dunstall, Chris Langford, Gary Ayres, Gary Buckenara, Chris Mew, Michael Tuck & John Platten were a few of their stars who became household names during this era.

More recently: while the Hawks did have a few poor seasons (by their lofty standards) in the late 1990s-early 2000s, they returned to the top in 2008 under coach Alastair Clarkson. They beat heavily-favoured Geelong for that year's flag, then went on to reach 4 consecutive Grand Finals between 2012-2015, dropping the first one to Sydney before winning the club's first hat-trick of premierships over Fremantle, Sydney and West Coast respectively. The Hawks really know how to step up during the finals.

The rest of the league should be grateful that the Hawks had a poor year in 2020. If recent history is any guide, Hawthorn will not be down for too long.

Re potential merger with Melbourne in 1996

In the mid-1990s the league was encouraging some of the Melbourne-based clubs to merge or amalgamate so that they would remain financially and competitively viable. Supporters of some of the smaller clubs were outraged that the league was openly discussing the elimination of 'their' club claiming that league administrators had grown out of touch with the sport's grass-roots supporter base. The ***Melbourne Hawks*** were a planned AFL team that would have involved a merger between the Melbourne and Hawthorn clubs at the end of the 1996 season. At the time, Hawthorn was in a lot of debt. Anti-merger movements led by Brian Dixon (Melbourne) and Don Scott (Hawthorn) eventually saw off the planned merger after weeks of meetings and spirited debate! Both teams retained their identity!

Rivalries

Hawthorn vs Geelong

For the last decade, the Easter round of footy has culminated with the Easter Monday match between Geelong & Hawthorn. Geelong beat the Hawks in the 1963 Grand Final but their rivalry only started to get intense from the mid-1980s. At Princes Park in 1985 Leigh Matthews struck Neville Bruns so hard that the latter broke his jaw. It was a particularly spiteful match with numerous reports. The umpires (who by the last quarter were struggling to control the game) missed the Bruns' incident as it happened off the ball. In extraordinary circumstances the police were later called to investigate and Matthews was de-registered as a player for a month and found guilty of assault in the Magistrates' Court. The unfortunate incident soured the end of his stellar playing career.

1989 Grand Final: Hawthorn 21.18.144 defeated Geelong 21.12.138

During the strange days of isolation in 2020, many footy fans took to watching some of the great matches from years gone by. The 1989 Grand Final between Geelong and Hawthorn was a classic! It was memorable for many reasons… Hawthorn equalled Melbourne's league record (set between 1954-60) by appearing in their 7th straight GF, it was the second highest scoring GF ever played and it featured an exciting last quarter comeback by the Cats which almost snared them their first premiership in 26 years. The 282 points scored on the day were second only to the 327 recorded in the 1972 GF between Carlton-Richmond. Gary Ablett kicked 9 goals in a losing cause. It was also the last VFL Grand Final played before the league changed its name to the AFL in 1990.

Even more than the high scoring, what really sticks in the memory of many fans is how violent this contest was. Geelong's Mark Yeates deliberately charged Dermott Brereton a moment after the ball was bounced to start the game leaving Dermie with broken ribs and in excruciating pain. Brereton refused to come off the ground despite the injury, kicked 3 goals for the game and inspired his team's win. Geelong was definitely 'playing the man' in an effort to unsettle the more skilful Hawks. Hawthorn's Robert DiPierdomenico, John Platten, Gary Ayres and Darren Pritchard also got very heavily crunched and by game's end they had only 13 fit players on the ground. Still it was back to back wins for the Hawks who confirmed their status as the dominant team of the 1980s (ahead of Carlton & Essendon).

Jump ahead 19 seasons and it was the Cats who entered the 2008 Grand Final as warm favourites to beat the Hawks. It wasn't to be however as wayward kicking in front of goal denied Geelong the chance to defend their premiership from the year before. The Cats' loss was only their second defeat all year - very painful for their supporters.

Since the 2008 GF, the rivalry between Geelong-

Hawthorn has grown in intensity and importance. Badly stung from losing the most important game of the year in 2008, Geelong won their next 11 games over Hawthorn, many of them by less than a kick. Almost all matches between these sides since 2007 have been played at the MCG, befitting of two teams that have dominated our competition for long periods over the last 14 years (between them, these two teams have won 7 of the last 14 flags). The Easter Monday clash is one of the most anticipated games of the year.

Great Indigenous Players

Cyril Rioli

Rioli was drafted at number 12 in the 2007 draft and made an immediate impact in his first season the following year, helping Hawthorn win the pemiership. Playing mainly in the forward pocket and also in the midfield, he went on to play in 3 more premiership-winning teams with the Hawks winning a Norm Smith Medal in the 2015 Grand Final. Like other great players from the Rioli family, Cyril had silky skills, could make 'something out of nothing' and most of all had an instinct for the game. He was never a high-possession player but really made his possessions count. He would chase/tackle, kick many important goals and could turn a game – he was that good! Injuries saw him retire in 2018 at age 28, having played 189 games.

Shaun Burgoyne (Port Adelaide, Hawthorn)

A fantastic player first with Port Adelaide and latterly with Hawthorn, Burgoyne has almost 400 games to his credit and won 4 premierships. He is used as a utility player in various positions. In 2009 he was vice-captain of Port and their highest-paid player when he surprisingly requested a trade and ended up going to Hawthorn. He became a critical player for the Hawks as they won a 'three peat' of premierships between 2013-2015. In the 2017 Doug Nicholls indigenous round, Burgoyne was given the honour of wearing a guernsey with the number '67', which signified 50 years since the 1967 Referendum which allowed indigenous Australians to be counted with the general population in the Census. Burgoyne is one of only two players to have played more than 150 games for two different clubs (a distinction he shares with Bernie Quinlan). He has also played the second-highest number of finals' matches in league history with 35 games to his credit (a number bettered only by Michael Tuck who played in 39 finals).

Burgoyne turned 38 at the end of the 2020 season and is currently the league's oldest player. He has played 389 games to date and has extended his contract with the Hawks through the 2021 season. If all goes well, he should become only the fifth player to notch 400 AFL games and if he keeps going for another 2 years, Brent Harvey's record of 432 games played could be under threat. The four players currently ahead of Burgoyne are: Harvey (432 games), Michael Tuck (426), Kevin Bartlett (403) and Dustin Fletcher (400).

Great Coaches

John Kennedy (Sr) Coached 19 seasons, 3 premierships. AFL Hall of Fame legend, Hawthorn captain 1955-59.

He is probably Hawthorn's 'greatest figure' as he is regarded as being the main man to have dragged the club out of the wilderness in the late '50s-early '60s and turned them into a powerhouse. His elevation in 2020 to Legend Status in the Hall of Fame which was shortly thereafter followed by his passing returned him to the spotlight. For many of us he is best remembered for his ***"Do Something"*** rant at his players at halftime during the 1975 Grand Final, which has been replayed a number of times. Kennedy experienced the highs and lows during his time with the Hawks. Joining the team in 1950 when they were the league's easy beats, the club failed to win a single game that year! A few years later in 1957 he was captain of the first Hawthorn team to *ever* reach the finals after 33 years in the VFL competition. Most significantly, in 1961 he had the distinguished honour of coaching Hawthorn to their first ever flag. "Kennedy's Commandos" were on the march - his passion, oratory and battered brown overcoat were inspirational to his players. He would coach the club to 2 more premierships in 1971 & 1976 before stepping down as head coach. He was lured out of retirement a decade later and coached North Melbourne for 5 seasons starting in 1985.

Allan Jeans Coached 26 seasons, 4 premierships (1 with St Kilda, 3 with Hawthorn), 62% winning percentage, AFL Hall of Fame.

In 1981 Jeans was hired as Hawthorn coach after David Parkin moved to Carlton. The Hawks would become the dominant team of the 1980s under his guidance. Under Jeans, Hawthorn won flags in 1983, '86 and '89 and were runners-up in 1984, '85 & '87. He would have won a fourth premiership with Hawthorn had he not spent a year out of coaching in 1988 due to health reasons.

David Parkin Coached 23 seasons, 3 clubs (Hawthorn, Carlton, Fitzroy), 4 premierships, AFL Hall of Fame.

He was the second player (after Graham Arthur) to captain a Hawthorn premiership side in 1971 and the second to coach a Hawthorn premiership team (after John Kennedy) in 1978. He was one of the first coaches to recognize the importance of closely analysing the strengths/weaknesses of the opposition - something which is taken for granted today. Post-football he has become a well-known media personality.

Alastair Clarkson Current coach since 2005, 4 premierships

He played 134 games over 11 seasons (1987-1997) for North Melbourne & Melbourne. Keen to step up to coaching after his playing days, he was an assistant coach at St Kilda and later Port Adelaide (2003-04) before being appointed senior coach at Hawthorn in late 2004. In his third season the Hawks were back in the finals and in 2008 they won their first premiership in 17 years with an upset victory over Geelong on Grand Final Day. The Hawks went on to win 3 flags in a row (2013-15) making Clarkson the most successful coach in the team's history. A man who is not afraid to speak his mind, Clarkson sometimes displays a fiery temper but he usually gets the best out of his players.

Great Goal Kickers

Peter Hudson (Hawthorn, 1967-74 & 1977) **727 goals**

In an incredible career playing in the VFL and TANFL, 'Huddo' kicked a total of 2,191 goals in 372 games – the most of any player. He just kept accumulating goals, including equalling Bob Pratt's record (set in 1934) of 150 goals in a season in 1971. His outstanding strike rate of 5.6 goals per game has him in pole position, just ahead of John Coleman on the all-time list. Hudson could read the play better than most and seemed to be able to sneak away from the opposition's full-back with great regularity. Once he did mark the ball, he was a really accurate kick. Sadly, he was also injury-prone or Gordon Coventry's league record of 1299 goals may well have fallen before 1999. Hudson had kicked 8 goals versus Melbourne at Glenferrie Oval in the first round of the 1972 season, when he landed awkwardly after taking a mark - he would not return to the field until Round 21 of the 1973 season. It was his only game that year and attracted much media interest. He was flown in from Tasmania just for the match (vs. Collingwood) and ferried by helicopter to VFL Park. Despite looking a bit 'proppy' he kicked 8 goals that day before returning immediately to Tasmania (he'd been working at a Norman Gunston gig at his Hobart pub on the Friday night)! After only 2 games in 1974, the knee injury flared again and he did not return to the VFL until 1977, when he completed a full season, kicking 110 goals and topping the goal kicking list for a fourth time. His goal kicking feats with Tasmanian club Glenorchy in the late 1970s were astonishing.

Leigh Matthews (Hawthorn 1969-85) **915 goals**

A truly outstanding player (and coach), 'Lethal Leigh' holds the record for most career goals by a non-full forward. He had a distinguished 332 game career with Hawthorn, won 4 premierships as a player, was their club captain for 5 seasons and won 8 club best & fairest awards (Peter Crimmins Perpetual Memorial Trophy). Matthews was rated by his coach John Kennedy as 'one of the two best players he ever coached at Hawthorn - equal with Graham Arthur'. On the field he was strong, quick and very hard to tackle. He had a reputation for giving and taking very hard bumps (hence the nickname 'Lethal'). Matthews is a legend in the AFL Hall of Fame.

Legacy: The Leigh Matthews Trophy is an annual award given by the AFL Players Association to the Most Valuable Player in the AFL. It is named in honour of Matthews, who won the inaugural MVP award in 1982. The trophy was first awarded, and all previous VFLPA/AFLPA MVPs were retrospectively given the Matthews Trophy in 2005.

Jason Dunstall (Hawthorn 1985-98) **1254 goals**

An absolute goal kicking machine, Dunstall is probably the best Aussie Rules footballer to come from Queensland. After winning a premiership for Coorparoo in the QAFL in 1984, he joined Hawthorn the following year and soon made his mark as one of our game's outstanding full forwards. He certainly wasn't the tallest player around (188 cm) but at 104 kgs he could outmuscle almost any opponent. He also had explosive speed which usually left defenders floundering - he managed to get clear to take chest marks a lot of the time as opposed to high grabs over packs. He played in 4 of Hawthorn's premiership sides and won the Coleman Medal 4 times. In 1992 he kicked 17.5 in a match against Richmond - the 17 goals ranking him equal second with Gordon Coventry (behind Fred Fanning) on the all-time list of most goals kicked in one game. Injuries took their toll on him during his last two seasons and he announced his retirement part way through 1998. At the time he and Tony Lockett both had a chance to break Gordon Coventry's long-standing career record of 1299 goals.

Lance 'Buddy' Franklin (Hawthorn 2005-13, Sydney 2014-) **944 goals**

He is the premier goal kicker of his generation and won his first two Coleman Medals while playing for Hawthorn in 2008 & 2011. His first 580 goals came during his 182-game stint with the Hawks and he won Goal of the Year honours in 2010 & 2013. Over the years Buddy has overcome numerous injuries and battled depression at times to notch 300 AFL games and reach 7th on the all-time list of VFL/AFL goal kickers. He has achieved All Australian selection 8 times in his storied career. When in full flight he is arguably the most exciting player in the competition to watch. Injury kept him off the field in season 2020 but fans will hopefully see him back in action next season.

Hawthorn's Team of the Century

B: *Gary Ayres, Kelvin Moore, Albert Mills*

HB: *Col Austen, Chris Mew, Peter Knights*

C: *Robert DiPierdomenico, Jim Bohan, Brendan Edwards*

HF: *Graham Arthur (Capt), Dermott Brereton, Gary Buckenara*

F: *Jason Dunstall, Peter Hudson, John Platten*

Foll: *Don Scott, Michael Tuck, Leigh Matthews*

Int: *Chris Langford, Ian Law, Roy Simmonds, Paul Salmon*

Coach *John Kennedy Sr*

Melbourne Demons

♪♩♪ *"It's a Grand Old Flag ..."* ♪♩♪

Variously known as the 'Redlegs', 'Fuchsias' and today the 'Demons' Melbourne is one of the world's oldest professional football clubs of any code. It was founded by cricketers in 1858 and the following year 10 codified rules were adopted for the game now known as Australian Rules football. Although Melbourne never won a VFA premiership they were one of the stronger teams and in 1896 became one of the 8 breakaway clubs to form the new VFL.

Two outstanding coaches: In the early years of the VFL Melbourne managed to win 2 premierships in 1900 & 1926 but usually didn't make the finals. However, the arrival of **Frank 'Checker' Hughes** as coach in 1933 saw a gradual reversal in fortunes and between 1939-1964 the club won 10 premierships! Early in his coaching career Hughes reportedly barked at his players, *"You are playing like a lot of flowers! Lift your heads and play like* ***demons****!"* The name stuck. In 19 years of senior coaching Hughes won 5 premierships including 1932 (with Richmond), '39, '40, '41 and 'the miracle of '48' with Melbourne. In 1948 top of the ladder Essendon had lost only 2 games all year and easily won the second semi over the Dees by 6 goals. However, in the first ever drawn Grand Final a fortnight later, Essendon completely squandered their chances by kicking a terrible 7.27.69 to draw the match with Melbourne who kicked 10.9.69. The following week the Bombers crumbled and Melbourne went on to record a comfortable win 13.11.89 to 7.8.50. Hughes retired after the 1948 season.

Norm Smith had played his 200th game for the

Demons during the 1948 season and was hoping to get the club's coaching job once Hughes stepped aside. Instead, he had to wait until 1952 to get the gig but when he did, he led the club through its most successful period winning 6 premierships (in 8 GF appearances) between 1954-64. Inheriting a team that had been 'wooden spooners' the previous year, Smith soon had Melbourne playing in the finals every season and overall, he compiled an impressive 70% winning record in finals' matches with the Demons.

Smith was a stickler for fitness & team discipline and his players were a very close-knit group that was the envy of all the other sides. Smith had several interesting nicknames including, 'Demon Dictator', 'Martinet of Melbourne' and 'Red Fox'! He also had an acid tongue which sometimes got him into trouble. In mid-1965 he was being sued by an umpire for defamation when he was sensationally terminated by the Demons before their Round 13 match. Although reinstated within a week he never again enjoyed the same relationship with Melbourne, though he did coach them for another two seasons. Smith's sacking, following as it did only a few months after Ron Barassi's dramatic move to Carlton were two of the biggest news stories ***ever*** in Australian football. Since this time Melbourne have never won another premiership.

Ron Barassi's name is synonymous with Australian Rules football and he is still recognized by many as the game's greatest identity. The Demons' 6 premierships in 10 years were as much inspired by Barassi on the field as they were by Norm Smith in the coach's box. Noel McMahen, John Beckwith, Frank 'Bluey' Adams, Brian Dixon, Stuart Spencer and Bob Johnson were other key players for the Dees during these years. Between 1955-60, the Demons won an impressive 6 minor premierships in a row, 11 of 13 finals matches and 5 flags!

1987 - first finals' appearance in 23 seasons: in Robbie Flower's farewell season, the Demons at last qualified for the finals for the first time since their 1964 premiership! To do so they had to win their final 5 games - their 15-point final round victory over the Bulldogs at the Western Oval was particularly memorable! The Demons were now on a mission - they demolished North Melbourne by 118 points in the elimination final, Sydney by 76 points in the first-semi-final before their dream was cruelly shattered in the preliminary final. After leading the Hawks all day at Waverley (helped by the wind changing direction at quarter time in the Dees' favour), Jim Stynes infamously ran over the mark which brought Hawthorn's Gary Buckenara within range to kick a dramatic long goal after the siren. Melbourne's Grand Final dream was over.

John Northey was the Demons' coach between 1986-1992, a period which saw them make the finals for five straight years. After their near miss in '87, Melbourne made it to the Grand Final in 1988 (only to lose badly to Hawthorn) and continued to do well for the next 3 seasons. They won at least one final's match each year in 1989, '90 & '91 but after a drop down the ladder in 1992, Northey left the club. Since then, a procession of coaches, including Neil Balme, Neale Daniher, Dean Bailey, Mark Neeld and Paul Roos have failed to bring the club sustained on-field success. Daniher was coach in 2000 when the Dees made it to their only other 'recent' Grand Final (losing to the all-conquering Essendon) and the club did make the finals a number of times during his 10-year coaching tenure. However, a good season or two also tended to be followed by a drop down the ladder. Under the coaching of Simon Goodwin, the Demons qualified for the finals in 2018 for the first time since 2006 and won through to the preliminary final before bowing out.

Jim Stynes (Brownlow Medallist 1991, Melbourne 'Team of the Century,' AFL Hall of Fame 2003)

Jimmy Stynes left an indelible mark on the Melbourne FC, the AFL and the wider community before his tragic death from cancer at age 45 in 2012. Growing up in Ireland and playing Gaelic Football and rugby union in his youth, he responded to an advertisement placed by the Melbourne Football Club in his local newspaper. The club was offering 2 scholarships to play football and study at university in Melbourne - his application was accepted and he arrived in Melbourne in November 1984 to begin a crash course in learning how to play Australian Rules football. He proved to be a quick learner and less than three years after arriving in the country, made his senior debut for the Demons versus the Cats in Round 16, 1987.

Throughout his playing career Stynes showed incredible courage, durability, determination, strength and most of all self-belief. His amazing run of playing in **244 consecutive games** started in Round 18 1987. He surpassed Jack Titus' 53-year-old record of 202 straight games in Round 9, 1996 and kept the streak going until early 1998 when a broken hand eventually ruled him out of the next game. To show how tough/courageous he was, consider that he played a number of games in 1993 with a chest guard to protect a compound rib fracture and in 1994 he played a few games despite having a medial ligament tear. He was one tough nut!

In 1991, Stynes became the first (and to date, the only) non-Australian born player to win the league's coveted Brownlow Medal. He retired after the 1998 season but continued to give back to his adopted sport and to the wider community in major ways.

In 1994 he co-founded The Reach Foundation in an effort to help and inspire young people. He worked on government advisory boards and for many years was a prominent youth worker himself. He was an author, was recognized as Victorian of the Year in 2003 and received an Order of Australia medal in 2007. The **Jim Stynes Medal** was first awarded in 1998 to the best Australian player in the **International Rules** series played between Ireland-Australia every second year.

In 2008 Stynes took over as Melbourne FC president

from Paul Gardiner and energetically set about turning the club's financial fortunes around - he started a drive called 'Debt Demolition' which quickly raised a lot of money and brought in many new members, including junior members. He also made it abundantly clear he did not support a proposal from some that the club relocate to the Gold Coast! Unfortunately, the Dees continued to flounder on the field and in July 2009 came the devastating news that Jim Stynes was battling cancer. True to form he kept working hard to help his club and others. By mid-2010 the club was debt-free. Stynes passed away in early 2012 and was given a State Funeral - befitting for such an exceptional Victorian.

Re potential mergers with Fitzroy and Hawthorn

The Melbourne football club has had its share of financial difficulties over the years, most notably in 1996 and again in 2008. At times the club considered merging with another club in order to survive.

1986: during this year consideration was given to a possible merger with Fitzroy (who were on very shaky financial ground). Nothing came to fruition.

1994: Melbourne & Fitzroy again discussed a merger.

Partly due to the failure of a meeting of minds on the naming of a new club, this merger did not get up.

1996: in the mid-1990s the league was actively encouraging some of the Melbourne-based clubs to consider a merger or amalgamation so that they could remain financially and competitively viable. Supporters of some of the smaller clubs were outraged that the league was openly discussing the elimination of 'their' club claiming that league administrators had grown out of touch with the sport's grass-roots supporter base. The ***Melbourne Hawks*** were a planned AFL team that would have involved a merger between the Melbourne and Hawthorn clubs at the end of the 1996 season (both clubs were heavily in debt at the time). Anti-merger movements led by Brian Dixon (Melbourne) and Don Scott (Hawthorn) eventually saw off the planned merger after weeks of meetings and spirited debate! Both teams retained their identity!

Great Goal Kickers

Fred Fanning (Melbourne 1940, 42-47) **411 goals**

At 193 cm and 102 kgs, Fanning was an imposing full forward for his era. He took VFL goal kicking honours

4 times during his short career (6.3 seasons) and is one of the few players to have a strike rate of 4 goals or better per game. Fanning is probably best remembered for scoring 18 goals, 1 behind vs Fitzroy in the final round of the 1947 season – this game turned out to be the final match of his VFL career. His tally is the most ever kicked by a single player in a VFL/AFL game and has stood the test of time for the last 73 years. In 1948 Fanning accepted an offer to captain/coach Hamilton in the western districts, earning a salary which was 3 times what the Demons had been paying him.

Allen Jakovich (Melbourne 1991-94, Footscray 1996) **208 goals**

A Demons' fan favourite, 'Jako's' debut season in 1991, got off to a rocky start and he was dropped after only 2 games. When he returned a couple of months later, he went on a tear and finished with 71 goals for the year. In the process he reached 50 goals in only 9 games - nobody in league history had *ever* booted 50 that quickly. He went on to equal John Coleman's record by kicking his 100th goal in only his 21st game the following season. While he was a goal kicking freak, his career was cruelled by a persistent back injury and fans were never able to see him show case his talents for an entire season. Friend John Coldham told me the following story about Allen Jakovich.

"One of the best things I've ever seen on a football field was in a 1993 match at the MCG vs. the Eagles. Allen gave his brother, the great Glen, a big kiss at the half time siren. Glen was enraged and the brothers were fighting as they left the field. Allen was what used to be called mercurial. If he trained properly, he would've been one of the greats - but not as much fun."

Great Indigenous Player

Jeff Farmer (Melbourne, Fremantle)

Nick-named "The Wizard" for his uncanny ability to create goals out of nothing, Farmer played 7 seasons for both Melbourne and Freo. He was Melbourne's leading goal kicker three times and achieved All Australian selection in 2000. He played a total of 249 games and kicked 483 goals. Farmer was one of our game's most exciting players to watch but also got himself in trouble both on and off the footy field.

Great Coaches

Frank 'Checker' Hughes Coached 19 seasons with Richmond & Melbourne, 5 premierships (1 with Richmond, 4 with Melbourne).

A two-time premiership player with Richmond in 1920-21, Hughes took over the coaching reins at the club in 1927. He spent 6 years coaching the Tigers and won the flag in 1932. At the end of that season the Richmond club secretary moved to Melbourne and Hughes decided to follow. He was a tough disciplinarian who got results. When he took over a struggling Melbourne team in 1933, he sacked 13 players and the team gradually started to get better. He got rid of the 'Fuchsias' nickname and told his players to play like 'Demons'.

Norm Smith Coached 23 seasons (Fitzroy, Melbourne, South Melbourne), 6 premierships all with Melbourne, Hall of Fame Legend, AFL team of the century coach

Smith had a highly successful playing career with the Demons in the 1930s & '40s before finishing off his playing days as captain-coach of Fitzroy. He was the Dees leading goal kicker 4 times and played in 4 premierships under coach Checker Hughes. He spent 3 seasons with Fitzroy between 1949-51 until appointed to coach Melbourne in 1952. In his 16 years coaching the Dees, the club won 6 premierships finished runners-up twice and made the finals in 11 of those years. Smith finished his coaching career with South Melbourne (1969-72) and got them into the finals in 1970 - the first time the Swans had made the finals since 1945.

Ron Barassi Coached 23 seasons, 4 clubs (Carlton, North Melbourne, Melbourne, Sydney), 4 premierships, AFL Hall of Fame legend.

Barassi had won 2 flags at Carlton and 2 at North Melbourne, prior to re-joining his old team for a five-year coaching stint starting in 1981. However, in his first season coaching the Demons, they won only one game for the year! While there was no 'dream run' for Barassi during the years he coached Melbourne, he did help set the stage for the club's resurgence in the latter half of the 1980s under his successor John Northey.

Melbourne-Collingwood rivalry

This rivalry was particularly strong during the second half of the 1950s and up to 1964. These two teams met in 9 finals between 1955-1964. In 1955, '56, '58, '60 and 1964, Melbourne won the Second-Semi to advance straight to the GF. Collingwood had the longer journey to get to the GF as by losing the Second-Semi (which they always did) to the Dees, the 'Pies had to then win the Preliminary Final to get another crack at Melbourne in the GF. While the Magpies did lose 4 of those 5 Grand Finals, the one time that they famously beat the Demons in 1958 was the one they particularly cherish. By defeating the Dees in the '58 Grand Final, Collingwood denied Melbourne the chance to equal the 'Pies' league record of 4 consecutive premierships (1927-1930). This is a record that no other team has been able to equal or surpass in the last 90 years.

Melbourne's Team of the Century

B: *John Beckwith, Tassie Johnson, Don Cordner*

HB: *Noel McMahen, Gary Hardeman, Don Williams*

C: *Brian Dixon, Allan La Fontaine, Robert Flower*

HF: *Hassa Mann, Ivor Warne-Smith, Garry Lyon*

F: *Jack Mueller, Norm Smith, Percy Beames*

Foll: *Denis Cordner, Ron Barassi (Capt), Stuart Spencer*

Int: *Frank Adams, Albert Chadwick, Wally Lock, Laurie Mithen, Jim Stynes, Todd Viney*

Coach *Norm Smith*

North Melbourne Kangaroos

♪♫ *"Join in the chorus, sing it one and all..."* ♪♫

The club was founded in 1869 by local cricketers who were looking for a way to keep fit during the winter. They were an inaugural member of the VFA when it formed in 1877 but under the name of 'Hotham' - the club name changed for a decade from 1877-87 before changing back to NMFC in 1888. The club's training ground has been at Arden Street since 1882 and for many years they played their home games there. The club was rejected a number of times in its attempts to join the VFL and it took a full 29 years before they finally gained admission in 1925 (along with Hawthorn & Footscray). NMFC were the dominant force in the VFA between 1910-20 with multiple premierships and an unbeaten run of 58 games, including 49 straight wins!

Nickname: the club was widely known as *'The Shinboners'* until the 1950s. Whether the name came from their reputation to target the other teams' shins or because local butchers dressed up beef leg bones in club colours is debatable! Former North club president Phonse Tobin (1953-56) was instrumental in the adoption of 'Kangaroos' as the club's nickname - he regarded the name 'Shinboner' as being somewhat unsavoury and wanted a name/mascot that it could show with pride.

Golden Eras: the club found the step up to the superior VFL tough going and for the first 20+ years, they finished on/near the bottom of the ladder. Finally, in 1949 they won a minor premiership and in 1950 they played in their first Grand Final... but lost to the more experienced Essendon. Another 20+ years of mediocrity followed but starting in 1973 the team's fortunes changed very quickly! Ron Barassi took over as coach in '73 and for his 8 years in charge NM were always in contention. North made it to five Grand Finals in a row (6 including the 1977 draw!) between 1974-78, winning in '75 & '77. They had acquired a number of top players from other clubs including John Rantall (South Melb), Doug Wade (Geelong), Barry Davis (Essendon), Malcolm Blight (Woodville SA) and Barry Cable (Perth). These imports combined well with players like David Dench, Keith Greig (dual Brownlow Medallist) and Wayne Schimmelbusch making North one of the VFL's powerhouse teams of that era (along with Richmond, Hawthorn & Carlton).

Despite adding the Krakouer brothers in 1982 and recruiting the legendary John Kennedy to coach them starting in 1985 for five seasons, the club went through another lean period until 1994 when their second golden era began. Denis Pagan replaced Wayne Schimmelbusch as coach in 1993 and for the next 7 years the Kangas were always in the top 4. Wayne Carey became the league's dominant player and Glenn Archer was another big star. NM won premierships in 1996 & 1999 and might have won in 1998 but for its woeful kicking of 8.22.70 against the Crows on Grand Final day. Since the early 2000s North haven't been as competitive but their 'Shinboner spirit' is still very much there. North's Brent Harvey is the AFL games record holder having played in 432 matches before his retirement in 2016.

Friday Night Footy – North were the pioneers in 1985-86

Today fans expect that a Friday night football match will be one of the marquee matchups of the round and the Friday night time slot is much sought after. In 1985 however, night football was just a curiosity - the league scheduled virtually all matches on a Saturday afternoon. The MCG had installed light towers after the 1984 season and 2 matches were scheduled for a Friday night the following year. Neither the players, fans or VFL officials quite knew what to expect. In Round 1 of the 1985 season everyone found out, when 65,000+ spectators turned up to see North play Collingwood - there was clearly great interest in Friday night footy. In 1986, North played in all 6 Friday night fixtures and were known as the Friday night specialists. When the league started to expand from 1987, Friday night football quickly grew in importance.

1996: rival club Fitzroy was placed into administration

during the season and it was now clear the club could not play on. Merger talks with North Melbourne were well advanced to form a combined club called the North Fitzroy Kangaroos Football Club to commence the following year. The proposal did not go ahead, due to disagreements on the composition of the new club board and partly because North insisted on having a list of 54 players for the following season (which the other AFL Clubs would not accept). It was probably a good thing for the rest of the league that a merger between North Melbourne-Fitzroy did not proceed. Imagine the super-team which might have been created? As it was, North Melbourne were about to dominate the latter half of the 1990s in their own right - winning two flags and finishing runners-up once.

Great Indigenous Players

The Krakouer brothers - Jim & Phil

These two were AMAZING to watch. They were both prodigious football talents who came from Mt Barker, WA and joined Claremont in the WAFL in the late 1970s. After leading Claremont to the WA premiership in 1981, they moved east and signed with North Melbourne the following year. They set the VFL alight during the 1980s with their speedy and skilful play and when they were both on song, it was so entertaining to watch them go. Jim was the fiery one - he would plough in where many footballers with a stronger sense of self-preservation feared to tread! He also had a lot of trips to the tribunal which often cost his team. Phil was more even-tempered. They were one of the greatest brother-acts our game has ever known.

Barry Cable

For a player considered 'too small' by many (rejected even by WA powerhouse team East Fremantle) and too slow by some (notably Lou Richards), Cable certainly left his mark on the game. He is regarded as one of the greatest rovers in the history of Australian Rules football and played over 400 senior games for Perth, North Melbourne and East Perth between 1962-1979. During this time, he won 4 WAFL premierships, 3 Sandover Medals (WAFL Best & Fairest) 3 Simpson medals (WAFL Grand Final, Best on Ground), 7 club best & fairest awards for Perth and 2 VFL premierships with North Melbourne. Cable was an absolute champion. The story of his connection with North Melbourne is worth telling. In 1969 after achieving everything that was possible to achieve with Perth, Cable was keen to move east to play in the VFL. He joined North Melbourne and played with distinction for one season in 1970, winning North's best & fairest award. North were a struggling team at that point and took home the wooden spoon. Cable would have continued at North however a clause in his contract stipulated that North would have to pay Perth a whopping $71,000.00 if they were to retain his services. He headed home and had a further 3 successful seasons with Perth before returning to North Melbourne for 4 years (1974-77). By that stage North were building a competitive team coached by the legendary Ron Barassi. In 1972 North had collected another wooden spoon and managed only one win for the season. However, with Barassi at the helm starting the following year, they won 11 games and from 1974, when Cable re-joined NM, the club appeared in the Grand Final for each of his four years. The Kangaroos won their first ever premiership in 1975 and added a second one two years later.

Great Goal Kickers

Doug Wade (Geelong, North Melbourne 1961-75) **1057 goals**

He initially tried out for Melbourne in 1960, but ended up joining Geelong the following season instead. A prolific goal kicker he became only the second player (after Coventry) to score 1000 goals or more in his career and still ranks fourth on the all-time list. He won 4 Coleman Medals 3 for the Cats, 1 for North) and played in 2 premierships (one for each team). In his last season (1975) North were hoping to finally win their first flag in club history but towards the end of the season Wade's form & fitness were diminishing. He begged Barassi and the selectors to name him in the GF team. They did so. Wade rewarded their faith in him by booting 4 goals and providing inspirational leadership on the field as the Kangas hopped to a 55-point win. It was a fitting end to a fabulous career.

Wayne Carey (North Melbourne, Adelaide 1989-2004) **727 goals**

Off the field Carey's indiscretions have been widely publicized/criticized, but on the field, he was the star player of the 1990s. In 1987 North made a token offer of $10,000.00 to the Sydney Swans (Carey had lived in Wagga Wagga so was zoned to the Swans) which was accepted. Carey played only 5 games in his first season but from 1990 he began making an impact and was made captain in 1992 at age 21 (the second youngest player to ever be appointed club captain). He was aggressive, took big marks and kicked long in his half-forward key position role. He also had many trips to the tribunal when his aggression went too far and spent a lot of weeks on the sidelines. He was one of few players down through the years who literally had the ability to win matches off his own boot - he was that good. During the 1990s, North Melbourne reached the preliminary final for 7 straight years, qualified for the Grand Final 3 times and won 2 premierships.

Great Coaches

Ron Barassi Coached 23 seasons, 4 clubs (Carlton, North Melbourne, Melbourne, Sydney), 4 premierships, AFL Hall of Fame legend.

Barassi left the Blues after the 1971 season to concentrate on his business career but by 1973 was back in the coach's box for North Melbourne. In 8 seasons with the 'Roos he won 2 premierships - the first two flags the club had ever won. He also led the club to 5 consecutive Grand Final appearances. Barassi later went on to coach Melbourne for 5 seasons and Sydney for 3 seasons.

Denis Pagan Coached 15 seasons, 10 with North, 5 with Carlton. Led North to 2 premierships, is NM's longest-serving coach and coach of their team of the century.

Pagan played 120 games for North between 1967-74, but was let go by Barassi after the team lost the '74 Grand Final to Richmond. Despite this, he would become a loyal servant to the *Shinboners* in a coaching capacity over many years. As coach of North Melbourne's Under 19s between 1983-91 he led the team to the Grand Final in all 9 years, winning 5 premierships. In 1993 he was appointed senior coach of the club where he made an immediate impact. In his 10 years at the helm, North won 2 flags, finished runners-up on another occasion and between 1994-2000, the Kangaroos played in 7 straight Preliminary Finals. Pagan achieved an impressive 62% winning average in his 240 games in charge of North and his team only missed the finals on one occasion.

The 10 Year Rule or, how North Melbourne won their first premiership!

In August 1972 the VFL introduced this rule as they were concerned about "restraint of trade" threats that were occurring in NSW rugby league about this time. The rule allowed players who had given at least 10 years continuous service to one club, to transfer as a free agent to another club without a clearance. Interestingly, North voted against the introduction of the rule but within 48 hours of the rule being passed, North officials had interviewed all 22 players who were eligible to move. North Melbourne's power brokers Allan Aylett, Ron Joseph and Al Mantello, literally 'flashed the cash' to encourage the 3 players they most wanted, to sign with the Kangaroos. **Doug Wade** (Geelong), **Barry Davis** (Essendon) and **John Rantall** (South Melbourne) all switched to North Melbourne in time for the 1973 season.

Only 3 other players moved clubs during the short-lived 10 Year Rule, namely ***Adrian Gallagher*** *(Carlton to Footscray),* ***Carl Ditterich*** *(St Kilda to Melbourne) and* ***George Bisset*** *(Footscray to Collingwood). Interestingly, during the early part of 1973, the late Sir Maurice Nathan (then VFL president), took time out from a VFL dinner to attack players 'for their lack of loyalty!' In May 1973, the VFL announced that the 10 Year rule would be abolished - now saying they were concerned about rising wage pressures on clubs!*

Their presence, along with that of newly-recruited coach **Ron Barassi** saw North just miss the finals in 1973, then qualify for 5 consecutive Grand Finals from 1974-1978. The team won their first two flags in 1975 & 1977. Money talks! Each of these players was offered a $10,000 sign-on fee and $10,000 per season to play. Wade had never earned more than $3,000.00 per year at Geelong - he would have been content to finish his career with the Cats where he had been made team captain in 1972. North Melbourne were clearly the major beneficiaries of the 10 Year Rule and these three players made major contributions to help secure North its first premiership within 3 years in 1975. Wade & Davis both retired after the 1975 Grand Final, while Rantall returned to his original club, South Melbourne for a further 4 seasons.

Miscellany

Re Essendon's interest to move to Arden Street in 1921: Essendon's first preference was to move from the East Melbourne Cricket Ground to the North Melbourne Cricket Ground (Arden Street) as many of their players and supporters came from this area. The North Melbourne football club was all in favour as they saw such a move as a way for them to finally get into the VFL (many pundits predicted Essendon would have been taken over or rebranded had they been based there). The proposed relocation fell through when the VFA, who were desperate to retain their use of the North Melbourne ground, successfully appealed to the State Government to block the move.

Metropolitan zoning for the different clubs was introduced in 1915 (until 1991) and clubs were meant to only recruit players from their allocated zones. In 1925 when the VFL admitted Hawthorn, North Melbourne and Footscray, a major stumbling block was to get existing clubs like Essendon & South Melbourne to agree to give up some of their recruiting zone to Footscray & North Melbourne in particular.

North Melbourne's Team of the Century

B: *Glenn Archer, David Dench, Michael Martyn*

HB: *John Rantall, Ross Glendinning, Ted Jarrard*

C: *Keith Greig, Les Foote, Laurie Dwyer*

HF: *Malcolm Blight, Wayne Carey (Capt), Wayne Schimmelbusch*

F: *John Dugdale, Jock Spencer, Allen Aylett*

Foll: *Noel Teasdale, Anthony Stevens, Barry Cable*

Int: *Brent Croswell, Barry Davis, Peter Steward, Sam Kekovich, Brent Harvey, Jim Krakouer*

Coach *Denis Pagan*

Port Adelaide Power

♪♩♪ "*We've got the Power to win...*" ♪♩♪

A bit of history: The Port Adelaide Football Club is the country's fifth oldest Australian Rules club and was founded in 1870. It is also Australia's most successful club having won 36 SANFL premierships between 1877-1999. The team has had particularly keen rivalries over the years with Norwood and Sturt. **Fos**

Williams and **John Cahill** were two highly successful coaches for Port, who won a combined total of 19 premierships for the club between 1951-1996. The accomplishments of each of these gentlemen has been recognized with their induction into the AFL Hall of Fame.

Dislike for Port Adelaide

They have a veritable army of their own raucous followers but non-Port supporters seem to have a particular dislike for the club. Why? One reason may be that they were simply too successful for very many years. Prior to entry to the AFL Port Adelaide were known as 'The Magpies' and wore a guernsey often referred to as 'The Wharf Pylon (and more recently 'Prison Bar') which is similar in appearance to that of Collingwood's guernsey. The 'Prison Bar' nickname originated from fans of the Norwood Football Club in the late 1980s and early 1990s "... in an attempt to deride the Port Adelaide supporter base, playing on Port Adelaide's strong working-class demographic. Supporters of Port Adelaide quickly adopted this insult as their own for the name of the guernsey. The 'Prison Bar' nickname eventually becoming part of the mystique and intimidation of the guernsey."

One journalist wrote in 2014

"'Prison Bars' has become a recent phenomenon, seemingly pushed - quite successfully – by those determined to cast the Port Adelaide image as an unsavoury part of society. Still, if it generates an image of fear, this will be taken as a compliment at Alberton (Port's training hub)."

When news of Port Adelaide's secret negotiations to join the AFL were made public in 1990, the 9 other SA clubs were outraged and saw it as an act of betrayal/treachery to the SANFL. Seven of the 10 SANFL clubs had lost money in 1989 and feared the loss of further income should Port leave the SANFL for the AFL. Port would have to wait a few more years to win a licence (1994) from the AFL to become the second South Australian team and it would be a further 3 years (1997) before they were able to take their place in the competition.

Entry to the AFL 1997

Admiration for Port Adelaide

Port is the only 'existing team' to join the AFL in the modern era. To do so they had to change their nickname (Magpies to Power), their guernsey & logo (required to incorporate teal and no vertical stripes to appease Collingwood) and their club song ('Power to Win'). Their inaugural captain was 1993 Brownlow Medallist Gavin Wanganeen, who returned home from Essendon to join his former club. The legendary John Cahill coached the Power for their first two seasons, before Mark Williams took over.

The Power qualified for the finals in their third year and by their 5th season recorded 16 wins, good enough for 3rd place after the minor rounds. The team then amazed most observers by winning the minor premiership for three straight years from 2002-04, a remarkable achievement for a team that had only joined the AFL a very few years earlier. *The only other teams to win 3 minor premierships in a row or more are: Essendon 3 (1999-2001), Geelong 4 (1951-1954), Collingwood 5 (1926-1930), Melbourne 6 (1955-1960).*

In 2004 Port fulfilled their promise and defeated the favoured Brisbane Lions in the Grand Final by 40 points. Byron Pickett, Gavin Wanganeen, Shaun Burgoyne and Warren Tredrea were standouts on the day and coach Mark Williams shed his 'choker' tag. The club again won through to the GF in 2007 but this time were humiliated by Geelong who won by a record GF margin of 119 points.

Since 2007 the team has mostly struggled, both on the field and financially. They did make it to a Preliminary Final 2014 when they lost by 3 points to eventual premiers Hawthorn. Chairman David Koch has been endeavouring to clear some heavy debts incurred by the club over the last few years. The hard work at the club resulted in a big-turnaround in the Covid-19 impacted 2020 season. Not only did Port win the minor premiership in the shortened 17 round season, they were top of the table after every single round - only the sixth time in the VFL/AFL's 124-year history that a team has accomplished this feat. Port lost a close Preliminary Final to Richmond which ended their 2020 campaign.

Note (interesting story): when Port Adelaide was awarded the licence to become the second South Australian team in the AFL, they were originally ***not*** expected to have any ongoing presence in the SANFL. Curiously, things did not work out that way as explained by former Port CEO Brian Cunningham - the excerpt below is from an interview he gave in 2018.

"I keep telling this story and I hope people listen.

When we tendered for the AFL licence, we got 99.9% of our members by survey [to answer] "do you want to go into the AFL?", [they replied] "yes we do, we want to be in the best competition and that best competition was the AFL". So, we go with a mandate from our members and we win the licence to go into the AFL. Port Adelaide Football Club was going into the AFL as the Port Adelaide Football Club and we had no intentions in our bid document to have a reserves side at that point in time or a presence in the SANFL because that was just too complex because of the politics. We couldn't imagine we could get one side in the AFL and have a second side in the SANFL. I can tell the story because it's true, I was there!

So, we win the AFL licence and then all of a sudden the opposition clubs in the SANFL start saying "What does that mean? Port have gone to the AFL... that means that we won't play them anymore! That means that their supporters won't come through the gates to watch our home games against Port anymore! Umm, we don't like that."

So, all of a sudden, the SANFL change the rules and say, "You can have the licence but one thing you have to do is (still) have Port Adelaide in the SANFL" and we said "Yep ok... well we're not going to fight that... but it wasn't the rules when you started the exercise."

Port Adelaide's team in the SA State League is still called 'The Magpies' as was historically the case.

Great Indigenous Players

Gavin Wanganeen (Port Adelaide, Essendon)

He was born in Mount Gambier, SA and had a distinguished career with the Port Adelaide Magpies in the SANFL, Essendon and Port Adelaide Power. Playing in various positions throughout his 300+ game career, he was a damaging on-baller, was sometimes used as a rebound defender and also could be a keen goal kicker. In 1993 he was a key member of Essendon's 'Baby Bombers' team which won the AFL premiership – he earned the distinction of winning the Brownlow Medal that same season. He returned to South Australia in 1997 to become the inaugural captain of the newly formed Port Adelaide Power. The Power quickly became one of the elite teams in the competition by the early 2000s, winning three minor premierships in a row (2002 to 2004) and their only premiership in 2004. This was the first "all-interstate" GF played between teams outside of Victoria. Wanganeen rose to the occasion by kicking 4 goals in his team's win over Brisbane... a victory which denied the Lions the chance to equal Collingwood's record of 4 consecutive premierships set between 1927-30. The 2004 Grand Final is also well-remembered for the animated post-game press conference given by winning coach Mark Williams, suggesting 'Allan Scott (head of Scott's Transport, Port's major sponsor) you were wrong' and that he (Williams) was not a choker!

Shaun Burgoyne (Port Adelaide, Hawthorn)

A fantastic player first with Port Adelaide and latterly with Hawthorn, Burgoyne has almost 400 games to his credit and has won 4 premierships. He is used as a utility player in various positions. In 2009 he was vice-captain of Port and their highest-paid player when he surprisingly requested a trade and ended up going to Hawthorn. He became a critical player for the Hawks as they won a 'three peat' of premierships between 2013-2015. In the 2017 Doug Nicholls indigenous round, Burgoyne was given the honour of wearing a guernsey with the number '67', which signified 50 years since the 1967 Referendum which allowed indigenous Australians to be counted with the general population in the Census.

Great Goal Kicker

Warren Tredrea (Port Adelaide 1997-2010) **549 goals**

Tredrea is Port's all-time leading goal kicker. He joined the Power in their inaugural season as an 18-year-old though he played only 1 senior game that year. Standing 194 cm tall and weighing 96 kgs, Tredrea quickly developed into one of the league's most imposing centre-half forwards starting in 1998. He played his entire career with the Power, won 4 John Cahill Medals (Port's best & fairest award), led the club's goal kicking list 8 times and was captain of their premiership winning team in 2004. Knee injuries interrupted his career several times. Tredrea was admitted to the AFL Hall of Fame in 2014.

Showdown Matches – Port Adelaide vs Adelaide

The team has a very fierce rivalry with cross-town rivals Adelaide - matches between the two teams are called ***The Showdown***, and Malcolm Blight refers to them as 'the greatest rivalry in football'. After 48 Showdown matches the ledger stands at 24 wins for each team! There are usually 2 Showdown matches each season.

Some history - why are these matches so intense?

South Australians take their football very seriously and their fans are very passionate/parochial. Back in 1990 as a result of their secret negotiations with the AFL, Port were expecting to be admitted to the AFL as the new South Australian team the following year. At the same time the Norwood FC (Port's bitter rivals in the SANFL) were also negotiating directly with the AFL to try to get *their* team admitted. The recently re-branded AFL was speaking to both of these teams separately because the SANFL were taking too long to commit to entering a South Australian side in the AFL. As explained in the earlier chapter about the Adelaide Crows, Port's bid was blocked in court and finally the SANFL 'came to the party' and quickly created a composite SA team. While Port Adelaide was awarded the second SA licence, they had to wait 6 extra years before their team could actually take the field. Given these circumstances it is hardly surprising that matches between the two clubs are played with a lot of feeling! Many would say the pride of South

Australia is at stake.

The Showdown is fun because you can expect the unexpected - ladder rankings are not a good indicator of which team will likely win. Over the years the team which was lower on the ladder has won the game about 1/3 of the time. The overall head-to-head differential between the two clubs has never been greater than 6 and they are currently level on wins after 24 years of head-to-head games! The teams have only once met one another in the finals - a Semi-Final played at Football Park in 2005 which Adelaide won by 83 points!

Some further Showdown stats

Closest Port Adelaide win: 4 points in 2013

Biggest Port Adelaide win: 75 points in 2020

Closest Adelaide win: 3 points in 2015 and 2018

Biggest Adelaide win: 84 points in 2017

Showdown Medal: a medal has been awarded since the 2000 season to the player adjudged to be best on ground. Multiple winners of this award include:

Port Adelaide: Robbie Gray (5), Josh Francou (3), Travis

Boak (2)

Adelaide: Mark Ricciuto (3), Sam Jacobs (3), Simon Goodwin (2)

Port Adelaide's Greatest Team (1870-2000)

B: *Dick Russell, John Abley, Ted Whelan*

HB: *Neville Hayes, Greg Phillips, Geof Motley*

C: *Craig Bradley, Russell Ebert, John Cahill*

HF: *Dave Boyd, Les Dayman, Harold Oliver*

F: *Scott Hodges, Tim Evans, Bob Quinn*

Foll: *Russell Johnston, Allan Reval, Fos Williams (Capt)*

Int: *Harry Phillips, Jeff Potter, Peter Woite, Lloyd Zucker*

Coach *Fos Williams*

Richmond Tigers

♪♪ *"Oh we're from Tiger Land..."* ♪♪

VFA years 1885-1907: the Richmond FC can trace their origins back to 1885. Richmond's Royal Hotel was the venue for a meeting that approved the formation of a club in February of that year. Club officials applied to and were given immediate entry to join the VFA that same season. For the first 15+ years the club struggled however and they were not invited to join the breakaway VFL in 1896. In the early 1900s Richmond's on-field results improved (2 flags in 1902 & 05) and the club started to build up a strong following. However, they also became openly at odds with the VFA who they felt should be doing more to curb on-field and off-field violence on match days as well as ungentlemanly conduct and poor sportsmanship in general. A low point was reached in 1904 when Richmond forfeited the VFA Grand Final versus North Melbourne as they were not happy with the selection of umpire Allen to officiate the game. Richmond also liked to organize practice matches against some of the VFL clubs... another thing which didn't endear them to VFA officials. In 1908 when the VFL was looking to expand its competition to 10 teams, Richmond were given the nod ahead of arch rivals North Melbourne and joined at the same time as the short-lived University club.

Early years in the VFL: the club won its first premiership in 1920 and backed it up by also winning the following year. The period 1920-44 was a very successful time for the club with 13 Grand Final appearances for 5 wins. Jack Dyer and Jack Titus were two of their biggest stars in the 1930s & '40s. Richmond developed particularly keen rivalries with their near neighbours Carlton and Collingwood which have endured through to the present day.

During the 1940 season Richmond playing legend Jack Dyer was one of many players who openly voiced his disapproval over the coaching methods of playing captain-coach Percy Bentley - feeling he should be replaced. Dyer threatened to move to the VFA after his father lost his spot on the Richmond board. Bentley retained his position as coach but the Tigers lost the GF that year to Melbourne - their champion player Dyer was tagged out of this game as former Tigers' coach Checker Hughes outcoached his counterpart. Bentley retired as a player after that season but when he asked for more money to stay on as coach of Richmond he was rebuffed. Bentley was incensed by this slight, left the club almost immediately and took over the coaching reins at arch-rival Carlton - adding further spice to an already fierce rivalry! Dyer took over as playing captain-coach of Richmond for the next 9 years, winning a flag in 1943. (Bentley went on to coach the Blues to two premierships).

Culture: in their VFA days, the club saw itself as a gentlemanly & sportsman-like club. As mentioned above, Richmond was very much against violence in the game and even sacked one of its players for using poor language! For this stance they were derided by some of the other clubs. The team's non-confrontational image in the early years can be partly attributed to two long-serving club presidents - George Bennett and Frank Tudor. Both were Richmond men and respected parliamentarians who took the view that how the game was played was more important than whether the game was won.

After World War I, the club's attitude hardened as they attempted to match it with the then power clubs Collingwood and Carlton. Over time the Tigers' approach to recruiting and training became more focussed on winning. After 20 lean years between the mid-1940s to the mid-1960s, the Tom Hafey era transformed Richmond into one of the most feared teams in the VFL. The club's football administrator, Graeme Richmond, drove this "win at all costs" mentality across the whole club, making the team a formidable force - which won five premierships between 1967 - 1980.

Lost years 1983-2012: Richmond fell on really tough times after losing the 1982 GF to Carlton. Poor recruiting, questionable financial decisions and too many coaching changes plummeted the team to the lower part of the ladder for the best part of 30 years -

in all those years the club only made the finals twice! Tony Jewell, one of the numerous coaches (to come & go) and the only one to be appointed for a second time, commented in 1986 that in the 4 years he had been away... "the supporters were gone, the members were gone and the money was gone - a real shame." The numerous coaches in the 1980s & '90s included: Francis Bourke, Mike Patterson, Paul Sproule, Tony Jewell, Kevin Bartlett, Allan Jeans, John Northey, Robert Walls, Jeff Gieschen - many of these were 'favourite sons' of the club, but when success didn't come, they came & went through the revolving door!

More recently: sustained on-field success started in 2013 and since Richmond broke their 37-year premiership drought in 2017, the Tigers have been the team to beat. They also won in 2019 & 2020! Brownlow Medallist Trent Cotchin has been an inspirational captain for the Tigers since 2013, and in 2017 Dustin Martin became the first player to win a Brownlow Medal, Norm Smith Medal and a Premiership Medal in the same season! The club has really prospered under the guidance of President Peggy O'Neal and CEO Brendon Gale and in 2018 became the first AFL club to have 100,000 members - the most of any Australian sporting team. Damian

Hardwick is in his 11th season as senior coach and the Tigers are roaring.

The club hosts the Korin Gamadji Institute (KGI) at Punt Road, which has delivered unique and innovative leadership and well-being programmes for young Indigenous boys and girls since 2008. In 2018, Richmond became the first sport's club to present at the United Nations Permanent Forum on Indigenous Issues.

Richmond vs Carlton Rivalry

The two clubs have had a long-standing rivalry based on geographic proximity and large supporter bases. Carlton was a founding member of the old VFL in 1896, while Richmond didn't join the league from the VFA until 1908. In the first half of the 20th century Richmond defeated Carlton twice in Grand Finals in 1921 and again in 1932.

Since 2008 the AFL has seen fit to stage the opening match of the season between these two clubs - a Thursday night fixture at the MCG which usually attracts a crowd of about 80,000 spectators. Matches between the two teams are regarded as 'blockbusters' - regardless of where they are on the ladder a large crowd can be expected. Richmond have completely dominated the head-to-head clashes in recent years and have not lost a game to Carlton since the 2013 elimination final. It is safe to say that there has been no match between Richmond-Carlton since the 1982 Grand Final that has been of genuine significance in terms of the race for the finals or the premiership.

My focus on the rivalry between these two teams is on the 16 seasons between 1967-1982 when virtually **all matches** between Carlton-Richmond were major fixtures with the result likely to have a bearing on the final outcome of the season!

1967-1982 - a golden era for the Tigers and the Blues

In the two decades preceding 1967 both teams had struggled and finals' appearances were rare. When fortunes changed, the change happened quickly and dramatically. During this 16 year stretch Carlton appeared in 8 Grand Finals (winning 6) while Richmond had 7 GF appearances for 5 wins - an excellent strike rate for both teams. They met one another in the premiership decider on 4 occasions (fully 25% of the time), each team winning twice.

In 1966 Richmond brought in one of their former

players Tom Hafey as coach. Hafey had been coaching successfully in Shepparton for a number of years and his impact at senior VFL level was almost immediate. 'T-shirt Tommy' quickly brought fitness and discipline to the club and during his 11 seasons at the helm, the Tigers won 4 premierships. It is no surprise that Hafey was named Richmond's 'Coach of the Century'. The Tigers had a 'kick long' and 'score often' approach. In 1967 they broke through for their first premiership since 1943 with a close, exciting win over Geelong.

Carlton had been in the doldrums all through the 1950s and into the '60s. In 1964 the Blues had one of their worst seasons (to that stage) ... finishing 10th in the 12-team competition. At the end of '64 new club president George Harris signed Melbourne legend Ron Barassi to cross to the Blues as player/coach starting in 1965. It was a master stroke. The transfer rocked the football world and remains to this day as one of the biggest player transfers in our game's history. Barassi's influence soon brought the Blues' success when they won their first flag in 21 years by edging Essendon in the 1968 Grand Final.

Memorable Finals' Matches

1969 Grand Final Richmond 12.13.85 defeated Carlton 8.12.60

Richmond only squeaked in to the final 4 in '69 by winning their last 4 games and ousting Hawthorn on percentage - each team finishing with 13 wins for the season. The Tiges certainly peaked at the right time and became only the third team to win the flag from 4th position. They swept through the finals, first demolishing Geelong by 118 pts in the elimination final, then ousting minor premiers Collingwood in the prelim. Defending champs Carlton entered the Grand Final as warm favourites having had the extra week's rest. The Blues rallied from 22 points down at the half to lead by 4 at the final change but the effort to overcome the deficit took a toll. Richmond finished over the top of them in the final quarter - Billy Barrot was the star for Richmond in this game. Have a look at You Tube to see one spectacular goal he kicked that day from way out on the boundary line!

1972 Second Semi Richmond 8.13.61 drew with Carlton 8.13.61

This game was one of few really close games between these two sides during this era. It was a scrappy affair at VFL Park. Richmond thumped Carlton by 41 points in the replay to move straight into the Grand Final. I checked a few of the match results from this era and was interested to see that first one team would win comfortably, then in the next match the other team would return the favour. An interesting statistic is that in the four Grand Finals featuring these two teams between 1969-1982, the underdog won each time!

1972 Grand Final Carlton 28.9.177 defeated Richmond 22.18.150

This ridiculously high-scoring match set a record for total points in a GF that still stands almost 50 years later (and is unlikely to be bettered anytime soon)! Carlton ruckman/coach John Nicholls masterminded Richmond's downfall in this game. Nicholls had taken over as coach after Barassi left (following the 1971 season) and scored 6 goals in this match. Robert Walls also kicked 6 while Alex Jesaulenko tallied 7. Incredibly the Blues had scored 114 points by halftime, led by 54 points at three quarter time and could coast to victory in the final term. Neil Balme kicked 5 goals for Richmond in a losing cause. Remarkably for a team of Richmond's quality the 1972 GF saw them concede the most points they had **ever** conceded in their history to that point. However, their losing score of 150 points also equalled the highest score ever previously scored in a Grand Final. It must have been an amazing game to witness in person!

1973 Grand Final Richmond 16.20.116 defeated Carlton 12.14.86

Carlton were pre-game favourites after defeating Richmond in the Qualifying Final but the Tigers were desperate to reverse the previous year's result. They adopted a very physical approach. At the 4-minute mark Richmond defender Laurie Fowler hit John Nicholls with a high shirt front which left the towering ruckman lying motionless on the ground for about 3 minutes! A hush fell over the crowd at this scary sight. Nicholls stayed out there but was pretty much dazed for the rest of the game, unable to effectively direct his team. Neil Balme king hit Geoff Southby in the second half and punched Vin Waite. Carlton were roughed up and down for the count. The Blues did not recover. The Tigers had entered the game with their champions Royce Hart and Francis Bourke under injury clouds but in winning the premiership cup ensured that it was an especially grand day for their faithful after their Under 19s and Reserves teams also won. A Tigers triple treat!

1982 Grand Final Carlton 14.19.103 defeated Richmond 12.13.85

Once again, these two teams met in two finals matches this year and once again the team with the easier path to the decider lost the big game. Richmond won the second semi comfortably by 23 points earning a week's rest. Carlton had to play Hawthorn in the prelim to earn a rematch with the Tigers. In the first 5 minutes of the GF as light rain fell, Carlton slammed on 3 quick goals to lead by 18 points - which was precisely their winning margin at game's end. Richmond recovered from their shaky start to lead by 11 points at the main change but the Blues took control in the third quarter - the premiership quarter as their coach David Parkin liked to say. This game is well-remembered because of the streaker who ran naked onto the pitch (and very close to Bruce Doull) during the third quarter!

The 1982 Grand Final marked the end of Richmond's golden era. They immediately nosedived after that and for the next 30 years only rarely made the finals.

In 2017 everything changed dramatically. Richmond have won three of the last four premierships and are the team to beat with a superb organizational structure and a huge fan base. The Tigers are roaring again.

Great Indigenous Player

Maurice Rioli

One of many terrific footballers from the Rioli family, Maurice was born on the Tiwi Islands, located a short distance off the coast from Darwin. He was a talented centreman with exquisite ball handling skills and lightning-quick reflexes. Rioli started his career in the mid-1970s with St Mary's in the NTFL before moving to South Fremantle in the WAFL where he starred between 1975-81. He helped lead South to 3 consecutive Grand Finals between 1979-81 (winning in 1980) and collected 2 Simpson Medals for best on ground performances in 1980 & 81. Switching to Richmond (1982-87) in the VFL, he made the move look easy by winning the Tigers' best & fairest in his first two seasons, winning the Norm Smith Medal for best on ground in the 1982 GF versus Carlton and placing second in 1983 to fellow West Australian Ross Glendinning in the Brownlow Medal. His best on ground performance in 3 consecutive Grand Finals in 2 different competitions may be a record?

Great Coaches

Percy Bentley Coached 22 seasons, 61% winning record in 414 games coached with Richmond & Carlton, 3 premierships (1 with Richmond, 2 with Carlton)

He was a strong ruckman and great tactician during his 16-year playing career with Richmond (1925-1940). Was captain-coach of the Tigers' 1934 premiership winning team. He moved to Carlton as coach between 1941-1955 and coached the Blues to two flags in 1945 and 1947.

Tom Hafey Coached 22 seasons, 4 clubs (Richmond, Collingwood, Geelong, Sydney), AFL Hall of Fame, coach Richmond Team of the Century, 4 premierships with Richmond, 64% winning percentage

Hafey had an unheralded 67 game playing career with Richmond during the 1950s but when he got his opportunity to coach the club in 1966, he really stepped up to the mark. He won 4 premierships in his 11 seasons at Tigerland. A fitness fanatic himself, Hafey was sometimes accused of working his players too hard on the training track, especially before important finals' matches. After leaving Richmond he coached Collingwood, Geelong and Sydney.

<u>**Damian Hardwick**</u> Head coach of Richmond since 2010 and has won 3 premierships with the Tigers

Hardwick is contracted to the Tigers until the end of 2021 and is set to surpass the legendary Tommy Hafey as the club's longest-serving coach during that season. He took over a struggling team in 2010 and over the last decade has built the Tigers into a powerhouse. They gradually got better each year (save for the blip in 2016) from 2010 to 2017 when he had the honour of coaching Richmond to its first flag in 37 years. There was great joy and relief in Tigerland after the long premiership drought was finally broken. Hardwick has really shown his coaching credentials since 2017 as the Tiges have continued right on with the job. The club's win in the historic 2020 Grand Final (under lights at The Gabba) has taken their tally to 3 flags in the last 4 years.

Hardwick had a successful 207 game playing career with Essendon and then Port Adelaide and won a premiership at both clubs. When he won the 2017 flag as head coach of Richmond Hardwick joined a very small & distinguished group who have won premierships as a player *and* coach for *3 different clubs* (the other three individuals are Ron Barassi, Mick Malthouse and Leigh Matthews).

Great Goal Kickers

Jack Titus (1926 - 43) **970 goals**

The Richmond spearhead thrilled crowds throughout his lengthy career with his spectacular goal kicking feats. Early in his career he mainly played as a flanker or in the forward pocket before being moved to full forward. Not just a fantastic goal kicker, Titus held the record for consecutive games played (202), a record which stood for 53 years until Melbourne's Jim Stynes bettered it in 1996. Until his injury in 1943 Titus looked set to become the second player (after Coventry) to kick 1000 goals and play 300 games. His injury caused him to miss Richmond's Grand Final victory that year and because of his age the club felt he should retire! While he gracefully accepted their decision, it was probably a poor one by Richmond - the following year they lost the Grand Final to Fitzroy by 15 points, when Titus' experience and goal scoring prowess may well have made the difference. Titus went on to play 1.5 years for Coburg in the VFA, booting 119 goals in 1945. He also loyally served the Richmond Football Club for 30+ years as a selector, Vice President, VFL delegate and as interim coach in 1965 for most of the season after Len Smith suffered a heart attack.

Legacy: in 1977 the VFL decided to issue an annual award 'in recognition of service to football at all levels.' Titus had been announced as the inaugural winner and after his tragic death shortly afterwards in early 1978 (he intervened in an altercation at his Limerick Castle Hotel) the award was named in his honour.

Kevin Bartlett (1965 - 1983) **778 goals**

KB had a distinguished 19 year playing career with Richmond, winning 5 premierships including a Norm Smith Medal in 1980. Also, in 1980, he surpassed John Rantall for the highest number of games played and by the time he retired at the end of the 1983 season, had become the first player to reach 400 games - his tally of 403 games is still the third highest in league history. Usually playing as a rover or a half forward Bartlett knew where the goals were and he currently sits in 13th position on the all-time list. He was given the nickname 'Hungry' as he appeared to want to kick the ball in preference to hand-balling it to his team mates. Bartlett won 5 Best & Fairest awards (Jack Dyer Medal) at Richmond during his career and in 2000 was duly elevated to legend status in the AFL Hall of Fame.

Matthew Richardson (1993 - 2009) **800 goals**

Richardson was recruited to the Tigers under the 'father-son' rule in 1992 - his father Alan was a key member of Richmond's 1967 premiership side. Richardson had great agility and with his towering height (197 cms) took an incredible 2,270 marks during his career. He also holds the record for most goals kicked at the MCG... 464. Richardson achieved All-Australian selection 3 times and led the Tigers' goal kicking list 13 times! His career unfortunately ended in Round 6 of the 2009 season at the SCG - he had kicked his 800th career goal early in that game before suffering a hamstring injury which caused him to miss the rest of the season. Richardson announced his retirement at the end of the year. His tally of 800 career goals currently has him in 12th position on the all-time list. Since his playing career ended Richardson has become a well-known football media commentator with the Seven network.

Richmond's Team of the Century

B: *Kevin Sheedy, Vic Thorp, Michael Green*

HB: *Basil McCormack, Gordon Strang, Mervyn Keane*

C: *Francis Bourke, Bill Barrot, Dick Clay*

HF: *Matthew Richardson, Royce Hart, Roger Dean*

F: *Dale Weightman, Jack Titus, Bill Morris*

Foll: *Roy Wright, Jack Dyer (Capt), Kevin Bartlett*

Int: *Des Rowe, Geoff Raines, Ian Stewart, Matthew Knights*

Coach *Tom Hafey*

Saint Kilda Saints

♪♪ "*When the Saints go marching in...*" ♪♪

While St Kilda has not had much on-field success during its long history the club does boast a large (over 40,000 members since 2017) & loyal fan base. The club did not win a VFA premiership but was one of the 8 breakaway clubs to form the VFL in 1896. The Saints have won 1 premiership (1966), been runners-up 6 times and won 3 minor premierships. Not a great return but they are also regarded as under-achievers because they have been 'wooden spooners' on 27 occasions. I will now concentrate on some of the club's highlights.

Allan Jeans: 'Yabby' was the Saints' most successful coach, a 'no-frills' coach renowned for being able to successfully motivate his players. He had an unremarkable 77 game playing career with St Kilda in the 1950s before making his mark as a coach. During his 16-year stint coaching St Kilda (1961-76) he took them to 3 Grand Finals in 1965, '66 and '71 and for his first 13 years in charge the Saints made the finals most of those years. Jeans only had 4 'losing' seasons. He cited 'burn-out' as his main reason for retiring at the end of 1976 before coming back rejuvenated in the 1980s to coach Hawthorn to 3 premierships. Jeans was an inaugural inductee into the Australian Football Hall of Fame in 1996 and is duly recognized as coach of St Kilda's 'Team of the Century'.

Brownlow Medallists: Colin Watson, Brian Gleeson, Neil Roberts, Verdun Howell, Ian Stewart, Ross Smith, Tony Lockett, Robert Harvey. Stewart & Harvey have the distinction of winning back to back Brownlow Medals for the club.

Tony Lockett: nicknamed 'Plugger', Lockett is the league's all-time goal kicking leader with 1360. He spent most of his career with the Sainters before moving to Sydney for his final five seasons. 898 of his goals were kicked during his 12 seasons with the Saints (1983-1994), the remaining 462 with Sydney. Lockett was co-winner (with John Platten of Hawthorn) of the Brownlow Medal in 1987 and to date is the only Coleman Medallist to also win the Brownlow Medal in the same year. Plugger won three additional Coleman Medals in 1991, '96 and '98. He is one of only 2 players (Jason Dunstall being the other) to kick 100 goals or more in a season, 6 times. Lockett was a formidable player.

1966 Grand Final: St Kilda 10.14.74 defeated Collingwood 10.13.73

This was the happiest day ever for St Kilda supporters. Most people know that Barry Breen's kick which wobbled through for a point late in the game won it for St Kilda. Even some trivia buffs may not know that this particular GF was the **closest ever played** - there was less than a kick in it at every change with the Saints leading by 4 pts at quarter time, Collingwood grabbing a 1-point half-time lead, before St Kilda got back in front by 4 points at the final change. There was never more than a 2-goal difference at any stage during this memorable match.

More recently: St Kilda went agonizingly close to winning both the 2009 and 2010 premierships under coach Ross Lyon but came up just short both times. In 2009 they led narrowly at every change in a game that was almost as close as the 1966 GF! In a brutal final term, Geelong managed to hold St Kilda goalless and were able to kick two late goals themselves, including one after the siren which extended the final margin out to 12 points.

The following year the Saints were up against Collingwood in the premiership decider. They played a strong second half to overcome a 4-goal halftime deficit and the game finished in a draw - only the third GF draw in league history (after 1948 & 1977). Unfortunately for Saints' fans, their team was completely outplayed by the 'Pies in the replay a week later and lost by 56 points.

After 5 years of coaching the club, Ross Lyon was

lured away by Fremantle at the end of the 2011 season. His sudden departure was considered contentious and upset a lot of people. He had led the club to 4 consecutive finals' appearances and is the club's second most successful coach after Allan Jeans. Interestingly, Lyon's side of the story regarding his abrupt departure from the Saints was only aired in mid-2020.

Silvio Foschini legal case 1983

Silvio Foschini was a teenage South Melbourne player who had a variety of reasons for ***not*** wanting to permanently remain in Sydney when the Swans moved north to the Harbour City. After an unhappy season in Sydney in 1982, he signed with St Kilda in 1983 but as he had not received a clearance from the Swans to do so, he felt compelled to take legal action. This was a high-profile case at the time with Foschini's legal team arguing that the VFL's clearance rules breached restraint of trade laws. Foschini won the case and was allowed to play for St Kilda. In handing down his judgement in the Victorian Supreme Court in 1983, Justice Crockett ruled that:

"the VFL's zoning, clearance, transfer & poaching rules were illegal" and "constituted an unreasonable restraint of trade on professional footballers."

Great Indigenous Players

Robert Muir (St Kilda, West Torrens, Woodville)

Those who followed the footy news closely in August 2020 would have read the tragic tale of a very talented football player. Robert Muir played 68 games in 10 years for the Saints, starting his VFL career under legendary coach Allan Jeans. Physically abused by his father when he was young and constantly racially abused on the footy field by opposition players and supporters, he found it hard not to fight back. After going public in August 2020 about the way in which he was racially vilified, both the AFL and St Kilda Football Club issued "unreserved apologies for the despicable way in which Muir was treated."

Nicky Winmar (South Fremantle, St Kilda, Western Bulldogs)

Winmar was a key member of St Kilda's resurgent team in the late 1980s/early 1990s, usually playing on the half-forward flank and sometimes on the wing. He played for 12 seasons with the Saints and won the club's best & fairest award (Trevor Barker Award) on two occasions. He was also selected twice to the All-Australian team, represented his home state of Western Australia on 8 occasions and was the first aboriginal player to play 200 AFL games. His fiery temper sometimes got the better of him. During his career Winmar was involved in several incidents of racial vilification. A photo of his response to one of these incidents in 1993 has been described as one of the most memorable images in Australian sporting history.

Great Goal Kickers

Bill Mohr (St Kilda 1929-41) **735 goals**

A deadly accurate kick for goal from any angle on the ground, Mohr led the league with 101 majors in 1936. He did not get the recognition he deserved as he toiled for a mediocre Saints' team that only made the finals in 2 of his 13 years (interestingly there were no 'wooden spoons' for St Kilda during those years either). He was an inaugural inductee into the AFL Hall of Fame.

Tony Lockett (St Kilda, Sydney 1983-99, 2002) **1360 goals**

His nickname 'Plugger' was inherited from his father &

grandfather, who both used to 'plug around in the garden'. Despite his large frame (191 cm/123 kgs), Lockett moved quickly & aggressively on the field, had sure hands and a big leap. He toiled for a St Kilda side that won the wooden spoon in each of his first 4 seasons with the club. 1987 was his breakout year in which he kicked 117 goals, won his first of 4 Coleman Medals and was co-winner of that year's Brownlow Medal with Hawthorn's John Platten. Lockett also helped lead St Kilda out of the wilderness and into the finals in 1991-92, for the first time since 1973. The Saints dropped back down the ladder again but when he moved to Sydney in 1995, he quickly became a cult figure in the Harbour City and helped attract many new fans to the game. In 1996 his after-the-siren point in the preliminary final against Essendon propelled the Swans into their first Grand Final in 51 years. The goals kept coming and in early 1999 Lockett overtook Gordon Coventry when he kicked his 1300th major in a match at the SCG versus Collingwood - this sparked one of the biggest pitch invasions ever. He retired at the end of that season and a 3-game comeback in 2002 saw only 3 more goals added to his record tally - that record may be safe for some years!

Great Coach

Allan Jeans Coached 26 seasons, 4 premierships (1 with St Kilda, 3 with Hawthorn), 62% winning percentage, AFL Hall of Fame.

One of our game's all-time great coaches he turned the Saints from a mediocre team into a powerful unit. He also led them to their only premiership in 1966. Jeans coached the club for 16 seasons between 1961-76 and was renowned as a master motivator. Jeans is by far and away the team's longest-serving coach, having been in charge for 332 games and achieving a 58% winning average with the club. He retired after the 1976 season citing burn-out as the main reason but returned in the 1980s to coach Hawthorn to 3 premierships.

Two Bizarre Matches of Recent Times

St Kilda have been involved in two of the most bizarre games in AFL history during the last 25 years and it is worth recounting them.

The night the lights went out... St Kilda vs Essendon VFL Park Round 10 1996

There were 43,925 fans in attendance at VFL Park on a

cold Saturday night in June to see the Saints take on Essendon. This was a home game for St Kilda as they had shifted their home matches from Moorabbin to VFL Park after the 1992 season. Late in the third quarter with play deep in the Essendon forward line, the lights suddenly went out and the ground was plunged into darkness. Initially the players were told that play would resume in about 15-20 minutes but at that stage nobody understood that there had been a major failure at a nearby energy substation and that the Waverley back-up generator had also failed. Many nearby suburbs were in darkness too. Chaos ensued as many spectators got restless and made their way onto the pitch. A couple of fires were lit on the ground and goal posts disturbed - mob mentality in the darkness! When an announcement was finally made at about 10:15 pm that the game would not continue people left the ground.

Aftermath: the AFL determined to finish the game 3 nights later by playing two twelve-minute halves. Essendon had been leading by 20 points when the lights went out and went on to win the game by 22 points. An impressive total of 17,590 spectators turned up on the Tuesday night to watch the end of the game, for free! At the time of the blackout the AFL had no rules in place as to what would happen in the event of a game having to be called off after it had started. Shortly after this unfortunate situation, the AFL brought in a new rule that stipulated should a game be abandoned *before* halftime in future, the game would be deemed a draw. If the stoppage happened *after* halftime, the team that was leading would be declared the winner.

Sirengate... St Kilda vs Fremantle York Park, Launceston Tasmania Round 9 2006

There was mass confusion at the end of this game when the umpires failed to hear the final siren and allowed play to continue. The umpires could be excused for not hearing the siren as the sound system was rather quiet, while the crowd noise was particularly loud due to the closeness of the match. Fremantle were leading by 1 point when the siren sounded but because the umpires hadn't heard the siren, play was allowed to continue for a further 25 seconds - enough time for St Kilda's Steven Baker to kick a point to level the scores. Fremantle coach Chris Connolly ran onto the ground to remonstrate with the umpires but the game was ***initially*** declared a draw.

Aftermath: Fremantle protested to the AFL and

fortunately common sense prevailed. After a four-hour sitting the AFL Commission overturned the original result and declared Fremantle the winner. Their stance was that in a modern-day competition, the team which is ahead at the end of the game, can't lose the game 25 seconds later!

Interesting note: the Sirengate game marked only the second time in the league's 110-year history that a result was overturned on appeal. The only other time this happened was in 1900 and also involved the Saints! A St Kilda vs Melbourne game that year finished in a draw... 68-68. The Saints however were successful in their protest which claimed that Melbourne had been incorrectly awarded a point which was kicked ***after*** the third quarter siren had sounded. Interestingly the success of their protest meant that the Saints finally had their *first ever* VFL win after three winless seasons! It was a most unusual way for St Kilda to achieve it. The win happened in front of their home fans at the Junction Oval in Round 1 and came after they had lost their previous 48 games! Unfortunately, this would be the team's only win for the season!

Did you Know? The VFL's oldest player?

Vic Cumberland's football career early last century took him to South Australia and New Zealand as well as Victoria. Early in his career he won a premiership with Melbourne in 1900 and later had three stints with St Kilda, including playing in their 1913 Grand Final team which lost a close one to Fitzroy. He served in World War I before returning to play with the Saints in 1920 at the age of 43. He is the oldest player to have played league football at the highest level.

In the modern era, Dustin Fletcher played his 400th and final senior game for Essendon in 2015 at the age of 40 years, 23 days.

St Kilda's Team of the Century

B: *Barry Lawrence, Verdun Howell, Kevin Neale*
HB: *Trevor Barker, Neil Roberts, Daryl Griffiths*
C: *Nicky Winmar, Ian Stewart, Lance Oswald*
HF: *Stewart Loewe, Darrel Baldock (Capt), Bill Mohr*
F: *Dave McNamara, Tony Lockett, Nathan Burke*
Foll: *Carl Ditterich, Robert Harvey, Ross Smith*
Int: *Barry Breen, Bob Murray, Alan Morrow, Jim Ross*
Coach *Allan Jeans*

Sydney Swans

♪♫ "*Cheer, cheer the red and the white...*" ♪♫

Sydney Swans (formerly South Melbourne)

The South Melbourne Football Club was founded in 1874 and won 4 VFA premierships between 1881-1890. The club broke away from the VFA at the end of the 1896 season to help form a new league, the VFL. Between 1874-1981, when the club shifted to Sydney, they played all their home games at the Lakeside Oval, in Albert Park.

Nickname: during the club's golden era in the 1930s

(they played in 4 consecutive Grand Finals between 1933-36) South recruited a lot of interstate players. Many of their 'foreign legion' came from Western Australia. An artist for the *Herald & Weekly Times* suggested the nickname '**Swans'**, as the black swan is the emblem of WA. The name stuck, in part due to the club's close proximity to Albert Park Lake.

Prior to this time, an unofficial nickname was 'The Blood-Stained Angels', shortened to 'Bloods'. The club colours are predominantly white (colour of angels) with a dash of red. In the early 2000s the playing group were looking for a word or phrase for the tough, accountable footy they wanted to play. 'Swans footy' was too sissy and someone suggested 'bloods football' because it sounded tougher and got back to the tradition of the very early years.

1945 'Bloodbath' Grand Final: Carlton 15.13.103 defeated South Melbourne 10.15.75

This infamous match between South Melbourne - Carlton was played in front of 63,000 spectators at Princes Park (hard to imagine so many people could squeeze in!). **It was the game's darkest day**. Fists & elbows were flying on and off the field, with players &

spectators knocked senseless! Ten players were reported and there should have been more reports. The game was an absolute disgrace which shook the football community to its core (and I expect the wider community as well).

Lean years: for the next 36 years until they moved to Sydney, the Swans fell on very hard times, making the finals only twice during this stretch. They did however win a few Brownlow medals along the way (the 14 Brownlow Medals won by Swans' players is easily the most number won by any team). In the late 1970s-early 1980s South was racking up large debts and by 1981 could not afford to fully pay their players.

Move to Sydney: at this very time the VFL was looking to extend the appeal of Australian Rules football to NSW & Queensland and wanted to establish a 13th team in Sydney. The South Melbourne board, recognizing the difficulties it faced with viability and financial stability in Melbourne proposed to the VFL in July 1981 that it play **all** its home games in Sydney in 1982. The VFL accepted the proposal. This initially caused great internal difficulties at the club but a spirited 'Keep South at South' campaign failed as the coach and players were all keen to relocate. In season

1982 the team was simply known as 'The Swans' before formally moving their operations to Sydney in 1983 and from that point onwards being known as the Sydney Swans.

The team had a couple of successful years in 1986-87 under the ownership of Dr Geoffrey Edelsten, coached by Tom Hafey and spear-headed by the flamboyant Warwick Capper (long blond hair, pink boots, tight shorts!). The good times didn't last and by the early 1990s the club was struggling once again to survive. The legendary Ron Barassi was lured out of retirement to coach for a couple of years and Tony Lockett was recruited from St Kilda in 1995. These moves quickly led to the club's revival in fortunes and brought the fans back. Since the mid-1990s the Sydney Swans have been one of the most consistent teams in the competition, appearing in 6 Grand Finals (for 2 wins) and finally ending their 72-year premiership drought in 2005. They have made the finals on all but six occasions since 1996.

Silvio Foschini legal case 1983

Silvio Foschini was a teenage South Melbourne player who had a variety of reasons for ***not*** wanting to permanently remain in Sydney when the Swans moved north to the Harbour City. After an unhappy season in Sydney in 1982, he signed with St Kilda in 1983 but as he had not received a clearance from the Swans to do so, he felt compelled to take legal action. This was a high-profile case at the time with Foschini's legal team arguing that the VFL's clearance rules breached restraint of trade laws. Foschini won the case and was allowed to play for St Kilda. In handing down his judgement in the Victorian Supreme Court in 1983, Justice Crockett ruled that:

"the VFL's zoning, clearance, transfer & poaching rules were illegal" and "constituted an unreasonable restraint of trade on professional footballers."

Great Goal Kickers

Bob Pratt (South Melbourne 1930-39) **681 goals**

He was an inaugural Legend of the AFL Hall of Fame and during his playing days in the 1930s was known for his spectacular high flying & diving marks. He set the league record for goals kicked in a season with 150 in 1934 (which was equalled by Peter Hudson in 1971). He kicked 10 or more goals in a match on 8 occasions, including a bag of 15 versus Essendon in

1934. He topped the VFL goal kicking list on three occasions. During Pratt's time with the club, South Melbourne experienced a golden era and played in 4 straight GFs between 1933-36. Pratt unfortunately missed the 1935 GF when he was clipped by a truck a few seconds after stepping off a tram in High Street, Prahran. He injured his ankle and suffered lacerations to both legs. The truck driver, who was a South Melbourne supporter, offered Pratt a packet of cigarettes by way of apology! Having beaten Collingwood comfortably in the second-semi a fortnight earlier, the absence of their great spearhead was obvious in the GF which they lost by 20 points to the Magpies. For the rest of his career Pratt was regularly plagued by this ankle injury, though he still kicked a lot of goals. This included his final two seasons with VFA club Coburg in 1940-41 when he kicked an incredible 263 goals in only 40 games. He was one of many VFL stars who moved to the VFA during their 'throw-pass era 1938-49'.

Lance 'Buddy' Franklin (Hawthorn 2005-13, Sydney 2014-) **944 goals**

Buddy won his third & fourth Coleman Medals while playing for the Swans in 2014 & 2017. In 118 games with Sydney, he has notched 364 goals which has taken him to 7th place on the all-time list of VFL/AFL goal kickers. After injuries derailed his 2020 season, football fans are hoping to see him return to the field in 2021 in pursuit of 1000 goals.

Great Indigenous Players

Adam Goodes

Goodes had an enviable record as a footballer for the Sydney Swans including: one Rising Star Award, 2 Brownlow Medals, 2 Premiership medallions, 4 times All Australian and member of the Indigenous team of the century. He displayed great courage in the 2012 Grand Final whilst playing with a serious injury, to help rally the Swans in the final quarter to victory over the Hawks. In 2014 he was awarded Australian of the Year honours for his efforts to end racism and for his work with indigenous youth community programs. Unfortunately, a booing saga in 2013 and all the attention the incident received afterwards, eventually forced Goodes to retire from the game 2 years later. In April 2019, on the eve of the premiere of the documentary film, *'The Final Quarter'*, about this controversy and how it affected Goodes, the AFL and all of its 18 clubs issued an unreserved apology for the sustained racism and events which drove Goodes out of the game.

Michael O'Loughlin

O'Loughlin became just the third indigenous player to play 300 AFL games and played his entire career for the Swans. He was their leading goal kicker in 2000-01 and an important member of their premiership winning side in 2005 - the first flag for the club in 72 years! He also achieved All-Australian selection twice and was duly inducted into the AFL Hall of Fame in 2015.

Lance 'Buddy' Franklin

He is the premier goal kicker of his generation and has won the Coleman Medal on 4 occasions (twice with Hawthorn, twice with Sydney). Injuries unfortunately prevented him from taking the field in the Covid-19 affected 2020 season but he has indicated he is keen to honour the last 3 years of his contract with the Swans during which time he hopes to get to 350 games and 1000 AFL goals. He certainly has the talent to do so provided his body holds up. Over the years he has overcome numerous injuries and battled depression at times to notch 300 AFL games and reach 7th on the all-time list of VFL/AFL goal kickers. When he is in full flight Buddy is the most exciting player in the competition to watch and I look forward to his return.

***** ***** *****

Focus on Roy Cazaly - the man and the song... 'Up There Cazaly'

Only one player can claim to have inspired Australian troops during wartime as well as inspiring a song which is our sport's unofficial anthem. He is also one of 12 'inaugural legends' inducted into the AFL Hall of Fame in 1996.

Roy Cazaly played 99 games for St Kilda (1911-20) and a further 99 for South Melbourne between 1921-27. He was the player that Carlton let get away in 1910! After injuring his shoulder in a Reserves' match for the Blues in 1910, he could not get the club's medical staff to treat his injury and decided to quit the team. He crossed to St Kilda starting the following year. During his years with the Saints, he won the club's best & fairest award in 1918 and was club captain in 1920. Due to internal troubles at St Kilda, he obtained a clearance to cross to South Melbourne in 1921.

At South he became the league's dominant ruckman and is considered by many to be the league's greatest player between the two World Wars! For a man who was only 180 cm in height, he possessed an incredible leap which enabled him to take fabulous marks and effect ruck hit-outs. Playing with rover Mark Tandy and ruck shepherd Fred 'Skeeter' Fleiter, the three were referred to as 'The Terrible Trio'. 'Skeeter' would regularly break up packs enabling Cazaly to have a clear run at the ball and it was Fleiter who first coined the phrase ***'Up There Cazaly'*** by yelling those words when he wanted Cazaly to rise high for the ball. South fans quickly started chanting the same words of encouragement. Cazaly attributed his leaping ability to constantly practising at home with a football suspended from a ceiling. Observers were often left in awe of his ability to 'hang in the air' longer than most players - Cazaly claimed to have developed the art of breathing to the extent that he would have more oxygen in his lungs, which in turn gave him added levitation. He was a player who stayed extremely fit and trained very hard.

Cazaly represented Victoria 13 times in the 1920s before moving to Tasmania in 1928 where he continued to play and coach. He represented Tasmania 5 times and periodically returned to Victoria. Altogether he played over 400 games in the two states and finished his playing career with VFA club Camberwell in 1941 at the age of 48. During World War II *'Up There Cazaly'* was used by Australian troops as a battle cry. Probably Cazaly's distinctive surname contributed to the phrase's enduring popularity.

In 1979 Mike Brady wrote/recorded the famous song called ***'Up There Cazaly'*** to help promote Channel Seven's coverage of the VFL. His Two Man band and others have performed the song many times since. Released independently on Fable Records, the Two-Man Band's recording of the song became the largest-selling Australian single released up to that time, with over 250,000 copies sold. Die-hard Aussie Rules fans probably know the words off by heart but for newcomers here are those words.

♪♪♪ Well you work to earn a living
But on weekends comes the time
You can do whatever turns you on

Get out and clear your mind
Me, I like football
But there's a lot of things around
When you line them up together
The footy wins hands down

Up there Cazaly
In there and fight
Out there and at 'em
Show 'em your might
Up there Cazaly
Don't let 'em in
Fly like an angel
You're out there to win

Now there's a lot more things to football
That really meets the eye
There are days when you could give it up
There are days when you could fly
You either love or hate it
Depending on the score
But when your team run out or they kick a goal
How's the mighty roar (hooray, hooray)

Up there Cazaly
You're out there to win
In there and at 'em
Don't let 'em in
Up there Cazaly
Show 'em your height

Fight like the devil

The crowd's on your side. ♪♪

Sydney's Team of the Century

B: *John Rantall, John Heriot, Vic Belcher*

HB: *Bill Faul, Ron Clegg, Dennis Carroll*

C: *David Murphy, Greg Williams, Herbie Matthews*

HF: *Tony Morwood, Laurie Nash, Gerard Healy*

F: *Bob Pratt, Tony Lockett, Paul Kelly*

Foll: *Barry Round, Peter Bedford, Bob Skilton (Capt)*

Int: *Bill Williams, Stephen Wright, Daryn Cresswell, Fred Goldsmith, Mark Bayes, Harry Clarke, Mark Tandy*

Coach *Jack Bissett*

West Coast Eagles

♪♫ *"We're the Eagles, we're flying high..."* ♪♫

The Eagles are one of Australia's most successful sporting clubs taking into account **all sports**, not just Australian Rules Football. Since joining the VFL/AFL in 1987 they have appeared in more Finals series than any other team, they have qualified for 7 Grand Finals in their 34-year history (winning 4) and produced 3 Brownlow Medallists. None of this in my mind is particularly surprising given the very strong football culture in Perth and the fact that WA has been producing outstanding footballers forever! In the early

1980s WA players including Ross Glendinning, Gary Buckenara, Simon Beasley, Maurice Rioli, Jim & Phil Krakouer, Ken Hunter, Peter Bosustow to name a few, all transferred from the WAFL to the VFL and all of them became stars. A $60,000.00 transfer fee was paid to the particular WA club by the Victorian clubs which helped keep some of those WA clubs financially viable.

Formation of the Eagles: in 1986 the VFL was in need of revenue. A few of the 12 existing clubs (especially Fitzroy) were struggling financially. In keeping with its aim to expand the game nationally the VFL was hoping to add 2 new clubs the following year (one in Brisbane, one in Perth). A license fee of $4 million was charged by the VFL per new team. It was a hard sell for the VFL to convince a majority of the existing clubs to accept the proposal. Many Victorian clubs were fearful of a WA 'Super Team'. In the short time between the VFL's idea being made public and the issuing of the license, Victorian clubs swooped. They enticed top players like Nicky Winmar, Mark Bairstow, Darren Bewick, Peter Wilson, Michael Christian, Craig Starcevich, Michael Mitchell, Earl Spalding and Paul Harding to move east. The Eagles on the other hand only managed to entice 4 WA born players to head back to Perth, most notably 1983 Brownlow Medallist Ross Glendinning.

While the team was being hastily assembled and the financials sorted out, the new club had to find a home ground (Subiaco) and it needed to find a spot to train. In 1986-87 they were training all over the place which was not easy! The $4 mil license fee was originally meant to be paid over 10 years but the VFL changed its mind and required it be paid by early 1987. Not everybody out west was happy with the name 'West Coast' instead of 'Perth' but there were too many issues regarding the naming of the club to be sorted out with existing WAFL teams.

Nobody knew quite what to expect from the Eagles in that first year but they gave us a good indication in their very first game, a home-opener versus Richmond at Subiaco. West Coast turned a 33-point three quarter time deficit into a famous/memorable 14-point victory. I have strong recollections of the 1987 season and remember watching that particular game on TV. The Eagles would go on to have a solid first year finishing just outside the 'Final 5' with a record of 11-11. They had started to soar. By 1991 in only their fifth season the Eagles held top spot for the entire season, finishing with 19 wins and only 3 losses. This was only the 4th time in AFL/VFL history that a team had held top spot on the ladder for the entire home & away season - the others being 1904 (Fitzroy), 1923 (Essendon) and 1953 (Geelong). *(This noteworthy achievement was later matched by Essendon in 2000 and Port Adelaide in 2020).*

West Coast had to wait another year before winning their first Premiership Cup and then made it 2 out of 3 by winning again in 1994. Peter Matera and Dean Kemp were the Eagles who won Norm Smith Medals in 1992 & 1994.

The Eagles never missed the finals in the 1990s and although they dropped off a little during the first decade of the current millennium, WCE still boast an exemplary record which is the envy of all the other clubs - they have qualified for the finals in 25 of their 34 seasons! That is a stunning 73% of the time since they joined the league.

Great Indigenous Players

Peter Matera

Matera had a splendid 13-year career with the Eagles,

playing 253 games and winning 2 premierships. He played on the wing, could really read the play well, was fleet afoot and had terrific goal sense. In the 1992 Grand Final, it was mainly thanks to Matera that West Coast rallied from a significant second quarter deficit to overrun Geelong and claim their first flag. He booted 5 goals from his wing position that day and duly won the Norm Smith Medal. Matera also achieved All Australian honours 5 times and was inducted into the AFL Hall of Fame in 2006.

David Wirrpanda

Wirrpanda was born in Melbourne and raised in Shepparton. He was picked up by the Eagles in the 1995 draft. He made his debut for the club the following year and to this day remains the youngest player to play at senior level for WCE (16 years, 268 days). Unfortunately, he was plagued by injuries during his first few seasons and it wasn't until the early 2000s that he cemented a regular spot in the team. He generally played in the back line but was sometimes moved forward to help his team. "Wirra" was an important player for the Eagles in their 2006 premiership victory. The year before he achieved All-Australian selection.

Great Goal Kicker

Josh Kennedy (Carlton 2006-07), West Coast 2008 -)
645 goals

Kennedy was drafted by Carlton at number 4 in the 2005 AFL draft but was traded to West Coast at the end of 2007 in the deal that saw Chris Judd move to Carlton. He soon established himself as the club's leading goal kicker. Kennedy has led WCE's goal kicking list on 7 occasions and is a two-time Coleman Medallist (2014-15). In 2018 he passed Peter Sumich to take over top spot on WCE's all-time goal kicking list. Kennedy was an important member of the Eagles' 2018 premiership team, kicking 3 goals in a low-scoring game which the Eagles rallied to win over Collingwood. At age 33 West Coast are hoping to get another good season or two from their imposing spearhead.

Great Coach

Mick Malthouse Coached 30 seasons (6 - Footscray, 10 - West Coast, 12 - Collingwood, 2.3 - Carlton), 3 premierships, most games coached 718

Malthouse joined the Eagles in time for the 1990 season and coached the team for the entire decade. During this time the team never missed the finals and won two flags in 1992 & 1994. As well as coaching the greatest number of senior games, Malthouse is the most successful finals' coach in history.

Rivalries

Their keenest rivalry is with their crosstown neighbours the Fremantle Dockers. WCE have always held a comfortable lead in matches between the two sides (known as the 'Western Derby') and as of season 2020, have won 31 games against 20 losses. In seasons 2005-06 WCE played 4 very closely-contested finals' matches against the Sydney Swans.

Thrilling Grand Finals (2005, 2006, 2018)

The Eagles have been in three really close GF games in the last 15 years, winning twice and losing once. The team met the Sydney Swans in consecutive years (2005-06) in both a Qualifying Final and a Grand Final - these 4 games were decided by a total of only 10 points and were as thrilling as they come!

In 2005 West Coast edged Sydney by 4 points in a Qualifying Final in Perth, which earned them an extra week's rest. When the teams met again 3 weeks later in the Grand Final, the Swans prevailed by 4 points. After establishing a 20-point halftime lead, Sydney only just held on to win their first flag in 72 years.

The following season (2006) saw the Swans win a qualifying final in Perth by 1 point, giving them the easier path to the decider where they again played the Eagles. This time it was WCE who built a solid halftime lead of 25 points, but then were forced to hang on grimly as Sydney staged a stirring fight back. Interestingly, both the Qualifying Final and the Grand Final in 2006 had the same score lines - 85-84. The Eagles' Chris Judd and Andrew Embley won Norm Smith Medals in 2005-06.

The 2006 GF was only the fourth in history to be decided by 1 point - Fitzroy over South Melbourne in 1899, Carlton over Essendon in 1947 and St Kilda over Collingwood in 1966 were the other three.

In 2018 West Coast played Collingwood in another close/tense GF. The Magpies recovered from losing their Qualifying Final to the Eagles, by beating GWS in a semi-final then soundly accounting for defending premiers and long-time rivals Richmond in a Preliminary Final. Collingwood had the lead in the Grand Final for over 90% of the game but after the 9-minute mark of the final quarter, the Eagles dominated. WCE however were feeling the pressure - dropping marks and missing a number of 'easy' set shots which would have put them in front. Finally, with less than 3 minutes remaining, Dom Sheed marked near the boundary line and converted the difficult set shot from about 40 metres out. The Magpies were unable to mount a final attack and WCE were the champs.

West Coast's Silver Anniversary Team (1987-2011)

B: *Michael Brennan, Darren Glass, David Hart*
HB: *Guy McKenna, Glen Jakovich, John Worsfold (Capt)*
C: *Chris Mainwaring, Ben Cousins, Peter Matera*
HF: *Brett Heady, Mitchell White, Chris Lewis*
F: *Tony Evans, Peter Sumich, Phil Matera*
Foll: *Dean Cox, Dean Kemp, Chris Judd*
Int: *Daniel Kerr, Don Pyke, Ashley McIntosh, Andrew Embley*

Coach *Mick Malthouse*

Western Bulldogs

♪♫ *"Sons of the West..."* ♪♫

Western Bulldogs (formerly Footscray Bulldogs up to 1996)

The club was founded in 1877 but didn't join the VFA until 1886. The 'team of the mighty west', played its home games at the Western Oval for well over 100 years but is now based at Marvel Stadium. Success was slow to come in the club's early years of VFA competition but in the last few seasons leading to the club's admission to the VFL in 1925, Footscray won 4 premierships between 1919-24.

At the end of the 1924 season Footscray played VFL champs Essendon in a charity match at the MCG - funds raised were for the benefit of Dame Nellie Melba's 'Limbless Soldiers Appeal'. Footscray scored a decisive 28-point victory over the Bombers and their win was instrumental in seeing the club admitted to the VFL the following year. Between 1918-24 there were only 9 teams in the VFL and this odd number meant that one team was assigned a bye each week. League officials were keen to address the issue and in 1925 added Footscray, North Melbourne & Hawthorn. The new 12 team competition would last for 62 years until West Coast & Brisbane joined in 1987. Footscray adopted the bulldog as its mascot in 1928 after a bulldog escaped from its owners and appeared to lead the team on to the ground for a home game against Collingwood. Supporters felt that the bulldog typified Footscray's "bulldog spirit" that season, and it became the club's nickname and mascot from then on.

Of the three new teams to join in 1925, Footscray did slightly better for their first 30 or so years. They won their first GF in 1954, well before the Hawks (1961) and North (1975). Generally-speaking however, the Bulldogs' fans have been very long-suffering. They have only appeared in 3 Grand Finals in 95 years and when they have had a strong season or two, they have struggled to consistently go on with it and make finals. It took until 2016 for the club to win a second premiership and that was certainly an unexpected result.

1961 Grand Final (Hawthorn 13.16.94 defeated Footscray 7.9.51): this was the first GF which *didn't* include one of the original VFL teams. Footscray had eliminated the powerful Melbourne team to get to the Grand Final but after leading at half time, ran out of legs in the second half and were overrun by Hawthorn. Interestingly, one of the Bulldogs' players later said, "...we just didn't hydrate. In those days we were told *not* to drink too much in case we got cramp."

1989 proposed merger with Fitzroy: discontent between players, officials and fans reached an all-time low in '89 and the club finished 13th. Club president Nick Columb was faced with the prospect of running a club with growing debt and declining membership & sponsorship. As a way forward he proposed a merger with Fitzroy which was also facing financial difficulties - the two clubs announced a merger and that the team would be called the **Fitzroy Bulldogs**. The merger never happened. Led by Peter Gordon and a number of others, funds were raised to pay off Footscray's debts. Doug Hawkins was the player folk hero of the faithful during these dark days.

1996 name change: the club changed its name from Footscray to the Western Bulldogs in an attempt to market the game more broadly in Melbourne's western suburbs. While the club has historically had rather low membership levels compared to other clubs, they achieved a record membership of 47,000+ in 2017, the year after winning their second-ever premiership.

2016 premiership victory: the club won an unexpected flag, coming from 7th place after the home-away matches to claim the title. They started their finals' run by travelling to Perth where they defeated West Coast by 47 points at Domain Stadium. They followed up with a semi-final win over triple defending premiers Hawthorn at the MCG and kept things rolling with a one goal victory over GWS in Sydney. While the finals-experienced Sydney Swans were appearing in their third GF in 5 seasons, the Bulldogs, under second-year coach Luke Beveridge, were not to be denied. On GF day they came home strongly in the second half to win the club's second ever premiership. Jason Johannisen, Tom Boyd and Liam Picken led the way for the Doggies, with Johannisen winning the Norm Smith Medal. The Bulldogs' victory ended a drought of 62 years for the club - during that time they had only qualified for one other GF. By winning in 2016, the Bulldogs became only the second team in AFL history to win four consecutive finals' matches to claim the title (after Adelaide in 1997). It was a massive relief for everyone associated with the club, as well as their loyal supporters, to achieve this victory.

Rivalry - Western Bulldogs vs GWS

In the last 5 years the Bulldogs have developed a fierce rivalry with the Greater Western Sydney Giants. In a very hard-fought 2016 preliminary final held at Giants' Stadium the Bulldogs came out on top by 6 points - a win which put them in their first GF since 1961. In 2019 the Doggies really needed a win in their away Round 22 clash against the Giants. They rose to the occasion magnificently and squeaked into the finals that year. Unfortunately, a fortnight later GWS turned the tables and convincingly won an elimination final between the two teams. The Bulldogs and Giants have a way of really niggling each other and their matches can sometimes be very heated!

Great Coach

Mick Malthouse Coached 30 seasons (6 - Footscray, 10 - West Coast, 12 - Collingwood, 2.3 - Carlton), 3 premierships, most games coached 718

He started his coaching career with the 'Dogs in 1984. In a career which spanned more than 30 years, his greatest achievement with Footscray was taking them to the preliminary final in 1985, where they lost by 10 points to eventual runners-up Hawthorn. Malthouse had premiership success with West Coast and Collingwood later in his career.

Great Goal Kickers

Bernie Quinlan (Footscray 1969-77 & Fitzroy, 1978-86) **817 goals**

'Superboot' was a prodigious kick who was the first player to play over 150 games for two clubs! During his 9 seasons at Footscray, he was mainly used as a centre-half forward but also played at centre-half back. He kicked 241 of his 817 goals in his 177 games with the Doggies.

Simon Beasley (Footscray 1982-89) **575 goals**

Beasley was recruited from West Australian team Swan Districts. He made an immediate impression for the Bulldogs kicking 82 goals for the club in an under-performing team in his first season. He was the club's leading goal kicker in 7 of his 8 seasons and averaged an impressive 3.7 goals per game. Beasley's best season was in 1985 when he won the Coleman Medal, booting 105 goals and helping lead Footscray to an appearance in that year's Preliminary Final.

Focus on Ted Whitten 'Mr Football'

Ted Whitten was regarded by his peers as the most naturally talented player of his era. He was far more than that to Footscray supporters and to thousands of people in Melbourne's western suburbs - put simply, Ted Whitten made people in the west feel better about themselves! If people elsewhere looked down upon the working classes in Melbourne's western suburbs, their answer during the Whitten years was,

'*We've got the best player*'! Whitten was a brilliant kick off both sides and a sure-handed mark. He played centre half-back and centre half-forward equally well and early in his career was a key member of Footscray's 1954 premiership winning team. 'Mr Football' was the playing captain-coach of his club for more than 10 years and stayed on for an extra season to coach Footscray after his retirement from playing in 1970.

He did experience conflict with the Footscray hierarchy at times and when he was replaced as coach at the end of the 1966 season, Whitten came very close to leaving the club and going to Richmond. The Bulldogs would not give him a clearance but he was fortunately convinced to return to play under his former team mate Charlie Sutton. He went on to notch up a league record 321 games. Whitten continued to contribute to our game as a commentator for many years and he was especially passionate about State of Origin football (having represented Victoria 29 times himself in interstate matches). His final public appearance in June 1995 was a memorable one - during a State of Origin match between Victoria-South Australia at the MCG, Whitten was driven for a lap of honour around the ground in a white convertible and received a standing ovation.

Legacy: Whitten was awarded an Order of Australia Medal in 1992 for his contributions to football. Such was his stature in the game that after his passing in 1995, 'Mr Football' was given a State Funeral and the Western Oval was renamed in his honour. A bridge on Melbourne's western ring road was also named in his honour. In 1996 he was one of 12 'Legends' inducted into the newly-opened AFL Hall of Fame.

Bulldogs' Brownlow Medallists

The club has won 10 Brownlow Medals since 1924, second only to Sydney and equal with St Kilda.

Allan Hopkins (1930), Norman Ware (1941), Peter Box (1956), John Schultz (1960), Gary Dempsey (1975), Kelvin Templeton (1980), Brad Hardie (1985), Tony Liberatore (1990), Scott Wynd (1992) and Adam Cooney (2008).

Hall of Fame Members

In addition to Ted Whitten, the following WB players have been inducted into the AFL Hall of Fame:

Gary Dempsey, Chris Grant, Doug Hawkins, Allan

Hopkins, Brad Johnson, Barry Round, John Schultz, Charlie Sutton, Norm Ware and Scott West.

The very first *WEG* footy poster marked the Bulldogs' premiership win in 1954

Each year an endearing footy image is produced which depicts the mascot of the flag-winning side with a gleeful grin/smile. Melbourne cartoonist William Ellis Green (WEG) drew the VFL/AFL's premiership poster for *The Herald* newspaper every year starting in 1954 until his passing in 2008. His first poster showed a very happy bulldog in 1954! By 1966 WEG's posters had become so popular that *The Herald* started producing and selling them (up to 100,000 copies) after the Grand Final. The tradition continues today thanks to artwork supplied by Green's private company.

Footscray/Western Bulldogs Team of the Century

B: *Charlie Sutton, Herb Henderson, John Schultz*

HB: *Wally Donald, Ted Whitten (Capt), John Jillard*

C: *Harry Hickey, Allan Hopkins, Doug Hawkins*

HF: *Alby Morrison, Kelvin Templeton, Chris Grant*

F: *Jack Collins, Simon Beasley, George Bissett*

Foll: *Gary Dempsey, Scott West, Brian Royal*

Int: *Jim Gallagher, Arthur Olliver, Brad Johnson, Norman Ware, Tony Liberatore, Scott Wynd*

Coach *Charlie Sutton*

The Finals

A look back at how the various systems operated

Background

From 1908 until 1971 **all** finals matches were played at the MCG, except between 1942-45 when the ground was unavailable due to World War II. (Princes Park was used in 1942, '43 and '45, with the Junction Oval being used in 1944). The VFL had to negotiate with the MCC to use the MCG for finals' football matches and weren't happy that the MCC held most of the negotiating leverage. When the VFL opened their own 80,000 seat stadium, VFL Park in 1970, they now had a new venue which was a viable option for finals' matches. Up until 1971 the VFL had been contracted to play all finals at the MCG. Once that contract expired, the league continued to have 4 finals at the 'G but by extending to a Final 5 system in 1972, were able to play the new Elimination Final and Second Semi Final at Waverley (VFL Park). In 1975 a new agreement shifted the Preliminary Final to VFL Park as well - an arrangement which lasted until 1990. Some readers will remember that in the late 1970s-early 1980s, the VFL pushed hard to also shift the Grand Final to VFL Park. Their attempts to do this were finally blocked by the Cain government at the end of 1983. From the late 1980s however, the thinking around the scheduling of finals started to change for two reasons. The league realized if it was to have a national competition, some finals' matches would need to be played interstate. Secondly, once the AFL and MCC had agreed to jointly fund the replacement of the MCG's aging Southern Stand (1992), the commercial desire for the AFL to schedule finals at VFL Park was reduced.

Argus Finals System - 1901-30

Named after the long defunct Melbourne newspaper, *The Argus*, the system involved a simple four-team tournament, followed by the right of the top ranked team from the home-and-away season to challenge for the premiership. First place after the home-away rounds would play third, second would play fourth with the winners to play off the following week. If the winner of that match was ***not*** the season's minor premiers, the minor premiers could challenge to determine who the Major Premier would be. There were up to 4 variations of the Argus System before it was ditched after the 1930 season. Throughout history there have been strong incentives for teams to perform well in the home-away rounds as the highest ranked teams have a better chance to win the premiership.

Page-McIntyre System - 1931-1971 4 teams 4 matches over 3 weekends

This new system was suggested by Richmond club secretary Percy Page and developed by Ken McIntyre. The system **did not** allow a challenge from the minor premier after all other finals' matches had taken place. Instead, the minor premiers and the second-placed team had the advantage of a "double chance" that permitted either team to lose their first finals' match without being eliminated. The number of finals matches was fixed at 4. In the first round of the Page–McIntyre system, the highest two ranked teams played each other (Second Semi-Final), with the winner going straight through to the Grand Final and the loser going through to the Preliminary Final. The lowest two ranked teams played each other (First Semi-Final) with the loser eliminated and the winner advancing to the Preliminary Final. The winner of the Preliminary Final went through to the Grand Final to play the winner of the Second-Semi.

McIntyre System - 1972-1990 5 teams 6 matches over 4 weekends

The top 3 teams after the home-away rounds all had a "double chance" and the top team (minor premier) had a week off during the first week of the finals. The fourth & fifth teams would meet in a cut throat Elimination Final. The second & third teams would play a Qualifying Final with the winner playing the minor premiers in the Second Semi-Final the following week. The loser of the QF would play the winner of the Elimination Final on the second weekend (First Semi-Final). The winner of this match would play the loser of the Second-Semi in the Preliminary Final during the third week of the finals. The Grand Final was played on the fourth weekend between the winner of the Preliminary Final and the winner of the Second Semi (the latter team always had an extra week's rest).

Ken McIntyre was again called upon to devise a Final 6 format (1991-93) and a Final 8 format (1994-99). Things got a bit more complex with an extra Elimination Final and more Qualifying Finals. The higher ranked teams still had a double chance but the system had its flaws and critics. In 1999 there was an uproar after West Coast was forced to play a 'home final' at the MCG (where they lost to Carlton) despite finishing higher on the ladder than the Blues. At issue also was the fact that the AFL was required to play at least one finals' match each weekend at the MCG as part of its contract - so West Coast missed out on hosting this match in Perth. Starting the following year, a revised Final 8 system of matches was introduced which is still the current model used today.

Today's Final 8 System (2000 -) 9 matches over 4 weekends

In the first week of the finals, 2 cut throat Elimination Finals are played with the 5th placed team playing 8th and the 6th placed team playing 7th. The losers are out.

Also, in the first week 2 Qualifying Finals are played between the 1st- 4th and 2nd- 3rd placed teams after the home-away rounds. The winners of these games get a week's rest in Week 2 of the finals. The losers have a double chance and get to play the winners of the two Elimination Finals in the Week 2 Semi-Finals. There are 2 Preliminary Finals held during Week 3 involving the 2 teams who won their Semi-Finals playing the winners of the 2 Qualifying Finals (who of course have had the 'advantage' of an extra week's rest). The winners of the Preliminary Finals square off in the Grand Final, which is contracted to be played at the MCG until 2058 - although in the Covid-19 impacted 2020 season the Grand Final was played at *The Gabba* in Brisbane.

Did you know... some fun Grand Final facts

1. During the 41 years of the Page-McIntyre final 4 system, only three teams won the premiership after finishing 4th in the home-away rounds. They were Carlton in 1945, Essendon in 1949 & 1965 and Richmond in 1969. Interestingly, no team ever won from third place!

2. Adelaide (1998) and the Western Bulldogs (2016) are the only two teams to win a flag after finishing in the bottom half of the 8 after the minor rounds.

3. In 2016 the AFL Commission decided that in the event of a 'tied' GF after four quarters, a full-game replay will *not* be played. Rather, extra time involving two 5-minute halves will be played to determine the winner.

4. The first 'All-Interstate' Grand Final was played in 2004 between Port Adelaide and Brisbane. The first GF featuring at least one interstate team was played in 1991 between Hawthorn and West Coast.

5. Season 2020 saw the first all-Victorian Grand Final since 2011 - the game was played at The Gabba in Brisbane. In the 31 seasons since the league changed its name to the AFL in 1990, there have been 10 all-Victorian Grand Finals and 3 all-interstate Grand Finals.

6. **Turnarounds**: during the 1931-71 period, the team which lost the second-semi, came back a fortnight later to win the Grand Final over the

same opponent, on 10 occasions! In 1957 there was a 77-point swing after Melbourne lost the second-semi to Essendon by 16 points, but beat the Bombers in the GF by 61 points!

Great Indigenous Footballers

Great Indigenous Footballers

The 2020 ***'Dreamtime at the 'G'*** match between Richmond-Essendon was played at Marrara Stadium in Darwin due to the Covid-19 pandemic and its serious impact on Melbourne. This match is usually the major fixture during the AFL's Indigenous Round, now called the **Sir Doug Nicholls** Round, designed to recognize and celebrate indigenous players & culture.

In this chapter you will read about some of the great indigenous footballers, starting with Sir Doug Nicholls.

Doug Nicholls (Northcote, Fitzroy)

Nicholls was born in NSW and became a prominent Aboriginal Australian from the Yorta Yorta people. He was a top athlete in the 1920s-30s, playing for Northcote in the VFA for a number of years (winning a premiership in 1929) before crossing to Fitzroy in the VFL for 6 seasons between 1932-37. Post-football, he became a Churches of Christ pastor and a pioneering campaigner for reconciliation. For Nicholls it was a very long lead-up (more than 30 years) to the 1967 Referendum which allowed the Commonwealth Parliament to **change the constitution** to make laws with respect to Aboriginal & Torres Strait Islander peoples. 90% of Australians voted 'Yes' at this referendum which also meant that Aboriginal people would be included in national censuses for the first time. Nicholls was knighted in 1972 and in December 1976 was appointed Governor of South Australia on the nomination of premier Don Dunstan.

The Krakouer brothers - Jim & Phil (Claremont, North Melbourne, St Kilda/Footscray)

These two were AMAZING to watch. They were both prodigious football talents who came from Mt Barker, WA and joined Claremont in the WAFL in the late 1970s. After leading Claremont to the WA premiership in 1981, they moved east and signed with North Melbourne the following year. They set the VFL alight during the 1980s with their speedy and skilful play and when they were both on song, it was so entertaining to watch them go. Jim was the fiery one - he would plough in where many footballers with a stronger sense of self-preservation feared to tread! He also had a lot of trips to the tribunal which often cost his team. Phil was more even-tempered. One of the greatest brother-acts our game has known.

Adam Goodes (Sydney)

Goodes had an enviable record as a footballer for the Sydney Swans including: one Rising Star Award, 2 Brownlow Medals, 2 Premiership medallions, 4 times All Australian and member of the Indigenous team of the century. He displayed great courage in the 2012 Grand Final whilst playing with a serious injury, to help rally the Swans in the final quarter to victory over the

Hawks. In 2014 he was awarded Australian of the Year honours for his efforts to end racism and for his work with indigenous youth community programs. Unfortunately, a booing saga in 2013 and all the attention the incident received afterwards, eventually forced Goodes to retire from the game 2 years later. In April 2019, on the eve of the premiere of the documentary film, **The Final Quarter**, about this controversy and how it affected Goodes, the AFL and all of its 18 clubs issued an unreserved apology for the sustained racism and events which drove Goodes out of the game.

Andrew McLeod (Port Adelaide SANFL, Adelaide)

He was born in Darwin and his original team was the Darwin Buffaloes. Fremantle had his rights in the AFL but on the eve of their first season in the competition traded away those rights to the Adelaide Crows in 1994 (no doubt something they later regretted!). McLeod went on to be an absolute superstar for the Crows and is their games' record holder having played 340 games for the club between 1995-2010. He was terrific in the mid-field, at half back or on the forward flank with his pace & agility. The Crows won back-to-back premierships in 1997-98 with McLeod starring in both finals' series and collecting Norm Smith Medals for best on ground in both of those Grand Finals.

Gavin Wanganeen (Essendon, Port Adelaide)

He was born in Mount Gambier, SA and had a distinguished career with the Port Adelaide Magpies in the SANFL, Essendon and Port Adelaide Power. Playing in various positions throughout his 300+ game career, he was a damaging on-baller, was sometimes used as a rebound defender and also could be a keen goal kicker. In 1993 he was a key member of Essendon's 'Baby Bombers' team which won the AFL premiership - he earned the distinction of winning the Brownlow Medal that same season. He returned to SA in 1997 to become the inaugural captain of the newly formed Port Adelaide Power. The Power quickly became one of the elite teams in the competition by the early 2000s, winning three minor premierships in a row (2002 to 2004) and their only premiership in 2004. This was the first "all-interstate" GF played between teams outside of Victoria. Wanganeen rose to the occasion by kicking 4 goals in his team's win over Brisbane, a victory which denied the Lions the chance to equal Collingwood's record of 4 consecutive premierships set between 1927-30. The

2004 Grand Final is also well-remembered for the animated post-game press conference given by winning coach Mark Williams, suggesting 'Alan Scott, you were wrong' and that he (Williams) was not a choker!

Maurice Rioli (South Fremantle, Richmond)

One of many terrific footballers from the Rioli family, Maurice was born on the Tiwi Islands, located a short distance off the coast from Darwin. He was a talented centreman with exquisite ball handling skills and lightning-fast reflexes. Rioli started his career in the mid-1970s with St Mary's in the NTFL before moving to South Fremantle in the WAFL where he starred between 1975-81. He helped lead South to 3 consecutive Grand Finals between 1979-81 (winning in 1980) and collected 2 Simpson Medals for best on ground in 1980 & '81. Switching to Richmond (1982-87) in the VFL, he made the move look easy by winning the Tigers' best & fairest in his first two seasons, winning the Norm Smith Medal for best on ground in the 1982 GF versus Carlton and placing second in 1983 to fellow West Australian Ross Glendinning in the Brownlow Medal. His best on ground performance in 3 consecutive Grand Finals in

2 different competitions may be a record.

Peter Matera (South Fremantle, West Coast Eagles)

Matera had a splendid 13-year career with the Eagles, playing 253 games and winning 2 premierships. He played on the wing, could really read the play well, was fleet afoot and had terrific goal sense. In the 1992 Grand Final, it was mainly thanks to Matera that West Coast rallied from a significant second quarter deficit to overrun the Cats and claim their first flag. He booted 5 goals from his wing position that day and duly won the Norm Smith Medal. Matera also achieved All Australian honours 5 times and was inducted into the AFL Hall of Fame in 2006.

Barry Cable (Perth, North Melbourne, East Perth)

For a player considered 'too small' by many (rejected even by WAFL powerhouse East Fremantle) and too slow by some (notably Lou Richards), Cable certainly left his mark on the game. He is regarded as one of the greatest rovers in the history of Australian Rules football and played over 400 senior games for Perth, North Melbourne and East Perth between 1962-1979. During this time, he won 4 WAFL premierships, 3 Sandover medals, 3 Simpson medals, 7 club best &

fairest awards for Perth and 2 VFL premierships with North Melbourne. Cable was an absolute champion. The story of his connection with North Melbourne is worth telling. In 1969 after achieving everything that was possible to achieve with Perth, Cable was keen to move east to play in the VFL. He joined North Melbourne and played with distinction for one season in 1970, winning North's best & fairest award. North were a struggling team at that point and took home the wooden spoon. Cable would have continued at North, however a clause in his contract stipulated that North would have to pay Perth a whopping $71,000.00 if they were to retain his services. He headed home and had a further 3 successful seasons with Perth before returning to North Melbourne for 4 years (1974-77). By that stage North were building a competitive team coached by the legendary Ron Barassi. In 1972 North had collected another wooden spoon and managed only one win for the season. However, with Barassi at the helm starting the following year, they won 11 games and from 1974, when Cable re-joined NM, the club appeared in the Grand Final for each of his four years. The Kangaroos won their first ever premiership in 1975 and added a second one two years later.

Graham 'Polly' Farmer (East Perth, Geelong, West Perth)

Few players can be identified as having "revolutionized" the way a particular position is played. Graham 'Polly' Farmer was one of those rare players. He was the outstanding ruckman of his generation with his attacking tap outs and he was also brilliant in his use of long handballs. It was said that until Farmer came along, handball was usually considered a 'last resort option' but he showed how it could become a 'dangerous offensive weapon'. Farmer was born in Fremantle and joined East Perth as an 18-year old in 1953. During the next 9 years the club won 3 WAFL premierships, while Farmer won 7 club best & fairest awards and 3 Sandover medals (WAFL's best & fairest award). He crossed to Geelong in 1962 but unfortunately was injured in the very first game and missed the rest of the season. In 1963 Farmer was instrumental in leading the Cats to the VFL premiership - this would be Geelong's last flag for 44 years! He finished equal second in the Brownlow medal count that season and won the club's best &

fairest in both 1963 and '64. Returning to Perth in 1968 he became player-coach for West Perth and in his four seasons won a further two premierships. After his playing days were over, he also coached both Geelong and East Perth during the 1970s. Farmer has been awarded Legend Status in the Australian Football Hall of Fame.

Lance 'Buddy' Franklin (Hawthorn, Sydney)

'Buddy' has had a distinguished career with two clubs... Hawthorn (2005-13) and Sydney (2014-). Playing in a key forward position he has been the league's leading goalkicker (Coleman Medallist) 4 times, been an All Australian 8 times and won 'goal of the year' honours in 2010 and 2013. Franklin currently sits in 7th position on the all-time AFL goal kicking list with 944 majors and is on track to become only the 6th player to reach the 1000 goal milestone in his career (after Tony Lockett, Gordon Coventry, Jason Dunstall, Doug Wade and Gary Ablett Snr). This is no mean feat in an era when kicking huge numbers of goals is mainly a thing of the past. In addition to his goal kicking feats, Buddy won 2 premierships while playing for the Hawks in 2008 and 2013. Franklin has sometimes been singled out for 'going missing' in important games, but when he is firing, there are few players in the game who are more exciting to watch.

Syd Jackson (East Perth, Carlton, Glenelg)

After a distinguished 5-year career with East Perth, Jackson was recruited by Ron Barassi and joined Carlton in 1969. He was a talented player who usually played in the centre or on the half-forward flank. In a distinguished 8-year career with the Blues he won two premiership medals in 1970 & 72. **Interesting story**: Jackson was lucky to play in the 1970 decider after being reported for striking Collingwood's Lee Adamson in the second-semi. He likely would have been outed for several weeks but the tribunal accepted Carlton's defence (devised by Blues' president George Harris with Jackson's approval) that his infraction was in response to a racial taunt. The tribunal exonerated Jackson who took his place in Carlton's team on Grand Final day. Twenty-two years later, Jackson admitted that there had been no racial provocation!

Cyril Rioli (Hawthorn)

Rioli was drafted at number 12 in the 2007 draft and

made an immediate impact in his first season the following year, helping Hawthorn win the pemiership. Playing mainly in the forward pocket and also in the midfield, he went on to play in 3 more premiership-winning teams with the Hawks winning a Norm Smith Medal in the 2015 Grand Final. Like other great players from the Rioli family, Cyril had silky skills, could make 'something out of nothing' and most of all had an instinct for the game. He was never a high-possession player but really made his possessions count. He would chase/tackle, kick many important goals and could turn a game – he was that good! Injuries saw him retire in 2018 at age 28, having played 189 games.

Jeff Farmer (Melbourne, Fremantle)

Nick-named "The Wizard" for his uncanny ability to create goals out of nothing, Farmer played 7 seasons for both Melbourne and Freo. He was Melbourne's leading goal kicker three times and achieved All Australian selection in 2000. He played a total of 249 games and kicked 483 goals. Farmer was one of our game's most exciting players to watch but also got himself in trouble both on and off the footy field.

Darryl White (Brisbane)

White has been a true role model for indigenous Australians for many years. He had a distinguished 14-year career with Brisbane between 1992-2005 and was a triple premiership player for the Lions. He won goal of the year honours in 1992. White could jump very high and took a number of spectacular marks during his career. He was mainly used in defence but because of his great leap and sure hands, was sometimes moved to other positions to help the team. He initially found the move from Alice Springs to Brisbane a difficult one, under hard task-master coach Robert Walls. At one training session which involved an 8 km cycle up a mountain, White hurled his bike off a cliff, telling his coach he had come to Brisbane to play football, not ride bikes!

Shaun Burgoyne (Port Adelaide, Hawthorn)

A fantastic player first with Port Adelaide and latterly with Hawthorn, Burgoyne has almost 400 games to his credit and won 4 premierships. He is used as a utility player in various positions. In 2009 he was vice-captain of Port and their highest-paid player when he surprisingly requested a trade and ended up going to Hawthorn. He became a critical player for the Hawks as they won a 'three peat' of premierships between 2013-2015. In the 2017 Doug Nicholls indigenous round, Burgoyne was given the honour of wearing a guernsey with the number '67', which signified 50 years since the 1967 Referendum which allowed indigenous Australians to be counted with the general population in the Census. Burgoyne is one of only two players to have played more than 150 games for two different clubs (a distinction he shares with Bernie Quinlan). He has also played the second-highest number of finals' matches in league history with 35 games to his credit (a number bettered only by Michael Tuck who played in 39 finals).

Burgoyne turned 38 at the end of the 2020 season and is currently the league's oldest player. He has played 389 games to date and has extended his contract with the Hawks through the 2021 season. If all goes well, he should become only the fifth player to notch 400 AFL games and if he keeps going for another 2 years, Brent Harvey's league record of 432 games played could be under threat. The four players currently ahead of Burgoyne are: Harvey (432 games), Michael Tuck (426), Kevin Bartlett (403) and Dustin Fletcher (400).

Leon Davis (Collingwood, Perth)

'Neon Leon' played most of his 12-year career with the Magpies as a small forward and later in his career was moved to defence. He earned goal of the year honours in 2008 and gained All Australian selection in 2009 and 2011. In the 2010 drawn Grand Final versus St Kilda he kicked a vital goal in the final term but otherwise had a quiet game. He was dropped for the GF replay but still received a premiership medal.

Dale Kickett (Fremantle with short stints at Fitzroy, WCE, St Kilda, Essendon)

A strong defender whose quick dash out of defence could electrify the crowd, Kickett played a total of 181 games, most of them for Fremantle between 1995-2002. He was initially drafted by Fitzroy but never could get settled in the big city of Melbourne. When he was traded to the Eagles in time for the 1991 season, he only managed 2 games - the Eagles already had a really strong list and Kickett was subsequently de-listed. He finally found his niche at Freo starting in their inaugural year under his former Claremont coach, Gerard Neesham. He is related to Derek Kickett and Buddy Franklin.

Michael O'Loughlin (Sydney)

O'Loughlin became just the third indigenous player to play 300 AFL games and played his entire career for the Swans. He was their leading goal kicker in 2000-01 and an important member of their premiership winning side in 2005 - the first flag for the club in 72 years! He also achieved All Australian selection twice and was duly inducted into the AFL Hall of Fame in 2015.

Nicky Winmar (South Fremantle, St Kilda, Western Bulldogs)

Winmar was a key member of St Kilda's resurgent team in the late 1980s/early 1990s, usually playing on the half-forward flank and sometimes on the wing. He played for 12 seasons with the Saints and won the club's best & fairest award (Trevor Barker Award) on two occasions. He was also selected twice to the All-Australian team, represented his home state of Western Australia on 8 occasions and was the first aboriginal player to play 200 AFL games. His fiery temper sometimes got the better of him. During his career Winmar was involved in several incidents of racial vilification. A photo of his response to one of these incidents in 1993 has been described as one of the most memorable images in Australian sporting history!

Indigenous Team of the Century

The team was announced in 2005.

B: *Chris Johnson (Fitz/Bris), Darryl White (Bris), Bill Dempsey (West Perth)*

HB: *Gavin Wanganeen (Ess/Pt Adel), Adam Goodes (Syd), Norm McDonald (Ess)*

C: *Peter Matera (Sth Freo/WCE), Maurice Rioli (Sth Freo/Rich), Michael Long (Ess/West Torrens)*

HF: *Nicky Winmar (Sth Freo/St K/West Bull), Stephen Michael (Sth Freo), Syd Jackson (East Perth/Carl/Glenelg)*

F: *Chris Lewis (Clare/WCE), Michael O'Loughlin (Sydney/Cent Dist), Jim Krakouer (Clare/NM/St K)*

Foll: *Polly Farmer (Capt) (East P/Geel/West P), Andrew McLeod (Adel/Pt Adel SANFL), Barry Cable (Perth/NM/East Perth)*

Int: *Michael McLean (Foot/Bris), Byron Pickett (NM/PA/Melb), Michael Graham (Sturt), David Kantilla (Sth Adel), Ted Kilmurray (E Perth), Peter Burgoyne (PA)*

Coach *Barry Cable*

Great Goalkickers

Great Goal Kickers

I like free-flowing, high-scoring games of footy more than low-scoring, defensive games which are common today. Seeing a player who can kick a 'bag of goals' is exciting and I'd say we remember our goal kicking heroes more readily than we do our outstanding full backs. My focus in this chapter is on the great goal kickers down through the years. Below are the *names* of the current top 20 VFL/AFL goal kickers of all time - followed, (in **bold**), by their total goals, number of games played and average goals per game in brackets. Reference will also be made to some players who ***are not*** in the top 20.

1. *Tony Lockett* 1360, 281 (4.8)
2. *Gordon Coventry* 1299, 306 (4.2)
3. *Jason Dunstall* 1254, 269 (4.7)
4. *Doug Wade* 1057, 267 (4.0)
5. *Gary Ablett (Sr)* 1031, 248 (4.2)
6. *Jack Titus* 970, 294 (3.3)
7. *Lance Franklin* 944, 300 (3.1) * still active
8. *Matthew Lloyd* 926, 270 (3.4)
9. *Leigh Matthews* 915, 332 (2.8)
10. *Peter McKenna* 874, 191 (4.6)
11. *Bernie Quinlan* 817, 366 (2.2)
12. *Matthew Richardson* 800, 282 (2.8)
13. *Kevin Bartlett* 778, 403 (1.9)
14. *Saverio Rocca* 748, 257 (2.9)
15. *Barry Hall* 746, 289 (2.6)

16. *Stephen Kernahan* **738, 251 (2.9)**

17. *Bill Mohr* **735, 195 (3.8)**

T18 *Peter Hudson* **727, 129 (5.6)**

T18 *Wayne Carey* **727, 272 (2.7)**

20.Harry Vallence **722, 204 (3.5)**

Dick Lee (Collingwood 1906-22) **707, 230 (3.1) Hall of Fame (1996)**

He played 17 seasons for Collingwood in the early 20th century. He was the first player to notch 700 majors and still holds the league record for being the leading goal kicker a total of 7 times. Lee was one of 136 players inducted into the AFL Hall of Fame when it was first established in 1996.

Gordon Coventry (Collingwood 1920-37) **1299, 306 (4.2) Hall of Fame Legend (1998)**

He joined the Magpies as Dick Lee's career was winding down and quickly established himself as the league's outstanding goal kicker for most of the 1920s-30s. He led the league in goals a total of 6 times, was the first player to ever kick 100 or more in a season (124 in 1929), was the first to kick 9 goals in a Grand Final (1928) and was the first to play 300 games. His record of 1299 career goals stood for 62 years before Tony Lockett surpassed it in 1999. Coventry won 5 premierships with the Magpies.

Jack Moriarty (Essendon, Fitzroy 1922-33) **662, 170 (3.9) Hall of Fame (2004)**

After only one season with Essendon, he crossed to Fitzroy where he had an outstanding 10-year career with the Maroons. Despite his diminutive stature (177 cm, 60 kgs), he had the ability to jump high over opponents and take strong marks. He led the league in goals in 1924 with 82 which was a league record at the time.

Jack Titus (Richmond 1926-43) **970, 294 (3.3) Hall of Fame (1996)**

The Richmond spearhead thrilled crowds throughout his lengthy career with his spectacular goal kicking feats. Early in his career he mainly played as a flanker or in the forward pocket before being moved to full forward. Not just a fantastic goal kicker, Titus held the record for consecutive games played (202), a record which stood for 53 years until Melbourne's Jim Stynes bettered it in 1996. Until his injury in 1943 Titus looked set to become the second player (after Coventry) to kick 1000 goals and play 300 games. His injury caused him to miss Richmond's Grand Final victory that year and because of his age the club felt he should retire! While he gracefully accepted their decision, it was probably a poor one by Richmond - the following year they lost the Grand Final to Fitzroy by 15 points, when Titus' experience and goal scoring prowess may well have made the difference. Titus went on to play 1.5 years for Coburg in the VFA, booting 119 goals in 1945. He also loyally served the Richmond Football Club for 30+ years as a selector, Vice President, VFL delegate and as interim coach in 1965 for most of the season after Len Smith suffered a heart attack.

Legacy: in 1977 the VFL decided to issue an annual award 'in recognition of service to football at all levels.' Titus had been announced as the inaugural winner, and after his tragic death shortly afterwards in early 1978 (he intervened in an altercation at his Limerick Castle Hotel) the award was named in his honour.

Harry Vallence (Carlton 1926-38) **722, 204 (3.5) Hall of Fame (1996)**

He had a stellar career with the Blues between 1926-36 and represented Victoria on 4 occasions. He was the league's leading goal kicker in 1931 but had a falling out with the club in 1936 after going interstate to represent Victoria. Upon his return he found that he had been demoted to the 'twos' to play centre half-back! He moved to Williamstown in the VFA as their captain-coach the following year. Fortunately, he was lured back to the Blues for the 1938 season, when he helped lead the team to their first premiership win since 1915. However, he moved back to Williamstown for a further three seasons from 1939-41. During this time, he won a VFA premiership (1939) and in May 1941 booted 20 goals versus Sandringham, bringing his total number of goals in both the VFL/VFA to over 1000.

Bill Mohr (St Kilda 1929-41) **735, 195 (3.8) Hall of Fame (1996)**

A deadly accurate kick for goal from any angle on the ground, Mohr led the league with 101 majors in 1936. He did not get the recognition he deserved as he toiled for a mediocre Saints' team that only made the finals in 2 of his 13 years (interestingly there were no 'wooden spoons' for St Kilda during those years either). He was an inaugural inductee into the AFL Hall of Fame.

Bob Pratt (South Melbourne 1930-39) **681, 158 (4.3) Hall of Fame Legend (1996)**

He was an inaugural Legend of the AFL Hall of Fame and during his playing days in the 1930s was known for his spectacular high flying & diving marks. He set the record for goals kicked in a season with 150 in 1934 (which was equalled by Peter Hudson in 1971). He kicked 10 or more goals in a match on 8 occasions, including a bag of 15 versus Essendon in 1934. He topped the VFL goal kicking list on three occasions. During Pratt's time with the club, South Melbourne experienced a golden era and played in 4 straight GFs between 1933-36. Pratt unfortunately missed the 1935 GF when he was clipped by a truck two nights before the game, after stepping off a tram in High Street, Prahran. He injured his ankle and suffered lacerations to both legs. The truck driver, who was a South Melbourne supporter, offered Pratt a packet of cigarettes by way of apology! Having beaten the Magpies comfortably in the second-semi a fortnight earlier, the absence of their great spearhead was obvious in the GF which they lost by 20 points. For the rest of his career Pratt was regularly plagued by this ankle injury, though he still kicked a lot of goals. This included his final two seasons with VFA club Coburg in 1940-41 when he kicked an incredible 263 goals in 40 games. He was one of many VFL stars who moved to the VFA during their 'throw-pass era 1938-49'.

Ron Todd (Collingwood 1935-39) **327, 76 (4.3) Hall of Fame (2017)**

Todd had a spectacular, albeit short 5-year career with the Magpies. His goal production went up each year culminating with him winning VFL goal kicking honours in 1938 & 39 when he booted 120 and 121 respectively. One of only 8 players to average better than 4 goals per game, he kicked 23 goals in the 1939 finals' series, a record which was not bettered for 50 years until Gary Ablett Sr kicked 27 in the 1989 finals. Todd was enticed to cross to Williamstown in time for the 1940 season at a time when the VFA had ended its player-transfer agreement with the VFL and was aggressively recruiting star players from the VFL. Not surprisingly, Todd made his mark in the rival competition, booting 672 goals in 7 seasons at Williamstown and establishing a league record of 188 majors in 1945, which still stands today. In 1997 Todd was initially selected in Collingwood's 'Team of the Century' but had his name removed when John McHale (Jock McHale's son) objected.

Fred Fanning (Melbourne 1940, 42-47) **411, 104 (4.0)**

At 193 cm and 102 kgs, Fanning was an imposing full forward for his era. He took VFL goal kicking honours 4 times during his short career (6.3 seasons) and is one of the few players to have a strike rate of 4 goals or better per game. Fanning is probably best remembered for scoring 18 goals, 1 behind vs Fitzroy in what turned out to be the final match of his VFL career in 1947. His tally is the most ever kicked by a single player in a VFL/AFL game and has stood the test of time for the last 73 years. In 1948 Fanning accepted an offer to captain/coach Hamilton in the western districts, earning a salary which was 3 times what the Demons had been paying him.

John Coleman (Essendon 1949-54) **537, 98 (5.5) Hall**

of Fame Legend (1996)

Despite his career being cut short by a knee injury after only 5.5 seasons, Coleman left an indelible mark on our game. Consider the following: he led the league in goals in 4 of his 5 full seasons; he scored 12 goals on debut in 1949 (including a goal with his first kick!) and kicked 100 for that season; while not overly tall (185 cm) he had this incredible ability to leap very high into the air from a standing start; he overcame a lot of hair tugging, head locks, thuggery & abuse generally by opposition players (and fans) who tried (usually in vain) to stop him. Long-time Essendon fans still loathe Carlton's Harry Caspar, who, on the eve of the 1951 finals provoked Coleman to such an extent that the star retaliated. Both men were suspended for 4 matches for striking, but for Essendon this meant that Coleman would be unavailable for the finals - they would go down to Geelong by only 11 points in the Grand Final. Coleman also proved to be an exceptional coach, guiding the Bombers to two flags (1962 & '65) during his 6 years at the helm.

Legacy: in 1981 the VFL decided to award a medal to its leading goal kicker for the home/away rounds, which it duly named the Coleman Medal.

Doug Wade (Geelong, North Melbourne 1961-75) **1057, 267 (4.0) Hall of Fame (1996)**

He initially tried out for Melbourne in 1960, but ended up joining Geelong the following season instead. A prolific goal kicker he became only the second player (after Coventry) to score 1000 goals or more in his career and still ranks fourth on the all-time list. He won 4 Coleman Medals (3 for the Cats, 1 for North) and played in 2 premierships (one for each team). In his last season (1975) North were hoping to finally win their first flag in club history but towards the end of the season Wade's form & fitness were diminishing. He begged Barassi and the selectors to name him in the GF team, which they did. Wade rewarded their faith in him by booting 4 goals and providing inspirational leadership on the field as the Kangas hopped to a 55-point win. It was a fitting end to a fabulous career.

Kevin Bartlett (1965-83) **778, 403, (1.9), Hall of Fame Legend (2000)**

KB had a distinguished 19 year playing career with Richmond, winning 5 premierships including a Norm Smith Medal in 1980. Also, in 1980, he surpassed John Rantall for the highest number of games played and by the time he retired at the end of the 1983 season, had become the first player to reach 400 games - his tally of 403 games is still the third highest in league history. Usually playing as a rover or a half forward Bartlett knew where the goals were and he currently sits in 13th position on the all-time list. He was given the nickname 'Hungry' as he appeared to want to kick the ball in preference to hand-balling it to his team mates. Bartlett won 5 Best & Fairest awards (Jack Dyer Medal) at Richmond during his career and in 2000 was duly elevated to legend status in the AFL Hall of Fame.

Peter McKenna (Collingwood, Carlton 1965-75, 1977)
874, 191 (4.6) Hall of Fame (1999)

Playing all but 11 games of his VFL career with the Magpies, McKenna's mop top hairstyle, genial grin and ability to take big marks and follow them up with goals made him our game's media star in the late 1960s/early '70s. He still holds the record for having scored at least one goal in 121 straight games. He won back-to-back Coleman Medals in 1972-73. In the 1970 Grand Final, McKenna had dominated in the first half, kicking 5 of his 6 goals as the Maggies surged to a 44-point halftime lead. Unfortunately, late in the second quarter he collided heavily with team mate

Des Tuddenham and was concussed. While he did finish the game, he had little influence in the second half as Collingwood faded - but for his concussion the outcome of that game may well have been different.

Peter Hudson (Hawthorn, 1967-74 & 1977) **727, 129 (5.6) Hall of Fame Legend (1999)**

In an incredible career playing in the VFL and TANFL, 'Huddo' kicked a total of 2,191 goals in 372 games - the most of any player. He just kept accumulating goals, including equalling the record (set by Bob Pratt) of 150 in a VFL season in 1971. His outstanding strike rate of 5.6 goals per game has him in pole position, just ahead of John Coleman on the all-time list. Hudson could read the play better than most and seemed to be able to sneak away from the opposition's full-back with great regularity. Once he did mark the ball, he was a really accurate kick. Sadly, he was also injury-prone, or Gordon Coventry's league record of 1299 goals may well have fallen before 1999. Hudson had kicked 8 goals versus Melbourne at Glenferrie Oval in the first round of the 1972 season, when he landed awkwardly after taking a mark - he would not return to the field until Round 21 of the 1973 season. It was his only game for the year and attracted much media interest. He was flown in from Tasmania just for the match (vs. Collingwood) and ferried by helicopter to VFL Park. Despite looking a bit 'proppy' he kicked 8 goals that day before returning immediately to Tasmania (he'd been working at a Norman Gunston gig at his Hobart pub on the Friday night)! After only 2 games in 1974, the knee injury flared again and he did not return to the VFL until 1977, when he completed a full season, kicking 110 goals and topping the goal kicking list for a fourth time. His goal kicking feats with Tasmanian club Glenorchy in the late 1970s were astonishing.

Leigh Matthews (Hawthorn 1969-85) **915, 332, (2.8), Hall of Fame Legend (1996)**

A truly outstanding player (and coach), 'Lethal Leigh' holds the record for most career goals by a non-full forward. He had a distinguished 332 game career with Hawthorn, won 4 premierships as a player, was their club captain for 5 seasons and won 8 club best & fairest awards (Peter Crimmins Perpetual Memorial Trophy). Matthews was rated by his coach John Kennedy as 'one of the two best players he ever coached at Hawthorn - equal with Graham Arthur'. On the field he was strong, quick and very hard to tackle.

He had a reputation for giving and taking very hard bumps (hence the nickname 'Lethal'). Matthews is a legend in the AFL Hall of Fame.

Legacy: The Leigh Matthews Trophy is an annual award given by the AFL Players Association to the Most Valuable Player in the AFL. It is named in honour of Matthews, who won the inaugural MVP award in 1982. The trophy was first awarded, and all previous VFLPA/AFLPA MVPs were retrospectively given the Matthews Trophy in 2005.

Bernie Quinlan (Footscray & Fitzroy, 1969-86) **817, 366 (2.2) Hall of Fame (1996)**

'Superboot' was a prodigious kick who was the first player to play over 150 games for two clubs! At Footscray he was mainly used as a centre-half forward but sometimes played at centre-half back. The Bulldogs were struggling financially during the 1970s and were forced to clear some of their better players to other clubs (Fitzroy paid $70,000 in 1978 to secure his services). In 1979 Quinlan announced to the club that he planned to return to work on his farm but when the team offered him a substantial pay increase, he relented and stayed for another 7 seasons until retiring after the 1986 season. By that point he had helped lead the Lions to their most successful post-war period and he became the club's first (and still their only) century goal kicker! I was very lucky to be visiting Melbourne in August 1983, attending the Round 21 match between Fitzroy-Collingwood at the Junction Oval on the day that Quinlan notched his 100th goal! He booted over 100 the following year as well and won the Coleman Medal both times. In 1981 Quinlan was a co-winner of the Brownlow Medal with South Melbourne's Barry Round - both players had started their careers with Footscray!

Gary Ablett Sr. (Hawthorn & Geelong, 1982, 1984-96) **1031, 248 (4.2) Hall of Fame (2005)**

Nicknamed "God" for his freakish all-round skills and ability to kick goals, Ablett joined Hawthorn in 1982 when he played 6 games, but never adjusted to big-city life. Ablett returned to country life the following year and then joined Geelong (for a $60,000 transfer fee) in 1984 for what turned out to be a very memorable 13-year career. Ablett played the majority of his career as a half-forward and when he turned it on, as he did during the 1989 finals' series, he was truly exhilarating to watch (he notched a record 27 goals in 4 finals' matches that season including a record-equalling 9 in the GF). Geelong coach Malcolm Blight put him at full forward starting in 1993. It was a move he relished and he won the Coleman Medal for three straight years between 1993-95, but the elusive premiership remained just that. A complex individual, Ablett became a born-again Christian in 1986 and wasn't particularly comfortable with the 'God' nickname bestowed upon him. He had numerous trips to the tribunal resulting in a number of suspensions. He retired in early 1991 but was talked into returning part way through the year.

Tony Lockett (St Kilda, Sydney 1983-99, 2002) **1360, 281 (4.8) Hall of Fame Legend (2015)**

His nickname 'Plugger' was inherited from his father & grandfather, who both used to 'plug around in the garden'. Despite his large frame (191 cm/123 kgs), he moved quickly & aggressively on the field, had sure hands and a big leap. He toiled for a St Kilda side that won the wooden spoon in each of his first 4 seasons. 1987 was his breakout year in which he kicked 117 goals, won his first of 4 Coleman Medals and was co-winner of that year's Brownlow Medal with Hawthorn's John Platten. Lockett also helped lead St Kilda out of the wilderness and into the finals in 1991-

92, for the first time since 1973. When he moved to Sydney in 1995, he quickly became a cult figure in the Harbour City. Lockett's presence helped attract many new fans to the game. In 1996 his after-the-siren point in the preliminary final against Essendon propelled the Swans into their first Grand Final in 51 years. The goals kept coming, and in early 1999 Lockett overtook Gordon Coventry when he kicked his 1300th goal in a match at the SCG versus Collingwood - this sparked one of the biggest pitch invasions ever. He retired at the end of that season and a 3-game comeback in 2002 saw only 3 more goals added to his record tally - that record may be safe for some years!

Jason Dunstall (Hawthorn 1985-98) **1254, 269 (4.7) Hall of Fame (2002)**

An absolute goal kicking machine, Dunstall is probably the best Aussie Rules footballer to come from Queensland. After winning a premiership for Coorparoo in the QAFL in 1984, he joined Hawthorn the following year and soon made his mark as one of our game's outstanding full forwards. He certainly wasn't the tallest player around (188cm) but at 104 kgs he could outmuscle almost any opponent. He also had explosive speed which usually left defenders floundering - he managed to get clear to take chest marks a lot of the time, as opposed to high grabs over packs. He played in 4 of Hawthorn's premiership sides and won the Coleman Medal 4 times. In 1992 he kicked 17.5 in a match against Richmond - the 17 goals ranking him equal second with Gordon Coventry (behind Fred Fanning) on the all-time list of most goals kicked in one game. Injuries took their toll on him during his last two seasons and he announced his retirement part way through 1998. At the time he and Tony Lockett both had a chance to break Gordon Coventry's long-standing career record of 1299 goals.

Stephen Kernahan (Carlton 1986-97) **738, 251 (2.9) Hall of Fame (2001)**

A South Australian native, Kernahan was initially signed by the Blues in 1981, but didn't join the club until 1986. He had a glittering 5-year career with Glenelg (1981-'85) in the SANFL, leading them to the 1985 premiership. He made an immediate impact upon joining the Blues in 1986 and after only 1 season, was appointed as club captain at the age of 23. He was highly regarded in this role for the next 11 seasons and holds the record amongst all AFL clubs of 226 games as club captain for one club. Kernahan topped the Blues' goal-kicking list 11 times in his career and he overtook Harry Vallence in his final season to become Carlton's all-time leading goal kicker. He represented South Australia 16 times in inter-state matches and is a member of the AFL Hall of Fame.

Wayne Carey (North Melbourne, Adelaide 1989-2004) **727, 272 (2.7) Hall of Fame (2010)**

Off the field Carey's indiscretions have been widely publicized/criticized, but on the field, he was the star player of the 1990s. In 1987 North made a token offer of $10,000.00 to the Sydney Swans (Carey had lived in Wagga Wagga so was zoned to the Swans) which was accepted. Carey played only 5 games in his first season but from 1990 he began making an impact and was made captain in 1992 at age 21 (the second youngest player to ever be appointed club captain). He was aggressive, took big marks and kicked long in his half-forward key position role. He also had many trips to the tribunal when his aggression went too far and spent a lot of weeks on the sidelines. He was one of few players down through the years who literally had the ability to win matches off his own boot - he was that good. During the 1990s, North Melbourne reached the preliminary final for 7 straight years, qualified for the Grand Final 3 times and won 2 premierships. Carey played 28 games with Adelaide at the end of his career.

Allen Jakovich (Melbourne 1991-94, Footscray 1996) **208, 54 (3.9)**

A Demons' fan favourite, 'Jako's' debut season in 1991, got off to a rocky start and he was dropped after only 2 games. When he returned a couple of months later, he went on a tear and finished with 71 goals for the year (in 14 games). In the process he reached 50 goals in only 9 games - nobody in league history had ever booted 50 that quickly! He went on to equal John Coleman's record by kicking his 100th goal in only his 21st game the following season. While he was a goal kicking freak, his career was cruelled by a persistent back injury and fans were never able to see him show case his talents for an entire season.

Matthew Richardson (Richmond 1993-2009) **800, 282 (2.8) Hall of Fame (2014)**

Richardson was recruited to the Tigers under the 'father-son' rule in 1992 - his father Alan was a key member of Richmond's 1967 premiership side. Richardson had great agility and with his towering height (197 cms) took an incredible 2,270 marks during his career. He also holds the record for most goals kicked at the MCG... 464. Richardson achieved All-Australian selection 3 times and led the Tigers' goal kicking list 13 times! His career unfortunately ended in Round 6 of the 2009 season at the SCG - he had kicked his 800th career goal early in that game before suffering a hamstring injury which caused him to miss the rest of the season. Richardson announced his retirement at the end of the year. His tally of 800 career goals currently has him in 12th position on the all-time list. Since his playing career ended Richardson has become a well-known football media commentator with the Seven network.

Matthew Lloyd (Essendon 1995-2009) **926, 270 (3.4) Hall of Fame (2013)**

Debuting at age 17 in the 1995 season, he had a distinguished career with the Bombers and is their all-time leading goal kicker. He was known for his strong over-head marking and his accurate left boot. On set shots from inside 50 he almost always converted and he also made quite a few from outside the arc. Lloyd won 3 Coleman medals in 2000, '01 and '03 and was a member of Essendon's all conquering premiership team in 2000. Lloyd is one of few players to register a goal with his first kick and in 2007 won 'Goal of the Year' honours for his back-heeled goal whilst surrounded by opposition players. He had a number of serious injuries over the years and decided to retire at the age of 31, shortly after the bump on Brad Sewell at the end of the 2009 season.

Lance 'Buddy' Franklin (Hawthorn, Sydney 2005-) **944, 300 (3.1)**

He is the premier goal kicker of his generation and has won the Coleman Medal on 4 occasions (twice with Hawthorn, twice with Sydney). Injuries prevented him from taking the field in the Covid-19 affected 2020 season but he has indicated he is keen to honour the last 3 years of his contract with the Swans during which time he hopes to get to 350 games and 1000 AFL goals. He certainly has the talent to do so, provided his body holds up. Over the years he has overcome numerous injuries and battled depression at times to notch 300 AFL games and reach 7th on the all-time list of VFL/AFL goal kickers. When he is in full flight Buddy is the most exciting player in the competition to watch and I look forward to his return.

Great Coaches

Great Coaches

In the 124 years of the VFL/AFL, the league has had a number of highly successful coaches. Coaching success is often measured by the number of games coached and premierships won. Here are the top 5 coaches overall in terms of games coached - I have also included number of wins and premierships next to their names.

Mick Malthouse - 718 games, 406 wins, 3 flags (2 West Coast, 1 Collingwood)

Jock McHale - 714 games, 467 wins, 8 flags (all with Collingwood)

Kevin Sheedy - 678 games, 389 wins, 4 flags (all with Essendon)

Allan Jeans - 575 games, 357 wins, 4 flags (1 St Kilda, 3 Hawthorn)

Tom Hafey - 522 games, 336 wins, 4 flags (all with Richmond)

In this chapter I am starting from way back when coaches often coached for 20+ seasons - something which doesn't happen too often in the modern era.

Jack Worrall 'The First recognized VFL coach'. Coached 18 seasons, 279 games, 59% winning average. (Carlton 8 years for 3 premierships, Essendon 10 years for 2 premierships).

He was one of Australia's great all-round sports' people of the late 19th century, being captain of Fitzroy in the VFA for 6 seasons and also playing for the club's cricket side. He was regarded as a more consistent footballer but after retiring from footy in 1894 continued to play cricket at the elite level, including playing 11 Test matches for Australia. He switched allegiances to join the Carlton Cricket Club in 1896 and finally finished his cricket playing career in 1902 at age 40. He was appointed secretary of the Carlton Football Club in 1902 and immediately set about leading training sessions, instructing players, formulating tactics and recruiting talent in a manner that created the role of club coach that is recognised today. For a number of years, he was often referred to as the club's "manager" or "secretary", until the term "coach" came into common usage. After retiring from coaching Worrall became a successful journalist in the 1920s & '30s.

Jock McHale Coached 38 seasons, 714 games, 66% winning average, 8 premierships in 16 Grand Finals - all with Collingwood. Legend status in the Australian Football Hall of Fame.

His name will forever be associated with his beloved Magpies. He played 261 games for Collingwood in the early 1900s and set the then league record of 191 consecutive games played between 1906-1917. He played in two premiership sides in 1910 and 1917 (the latter achieved while he was player coach). His remarkable longevity of 38 years coaching the team began in 1912 and between 1919-1936 he coached the Magpies to a further 7 Grand Final wins. McHale's total of 8 premierships as coach is still the league record. The Jock McHale Medal has been awarded to the winning Grand Final coach since the 2001 season. The medal was later retrospectively awarded to all the winning coaches between 1950-2000.

Notes: McHale was not at the ground on the day when the Magpies won their fourth straight flag in 1930, due to a bout of the flu. He is still given credit for that victory. In 1953 he helped Phonse Kyne and the Collingwood coaching staff plot the team's upset Grand Final victory over Geelong. After the win (which broke a 17-year premiership drought) he became extremely emotional. The next day he unfortunately suffered a heart attack and passed away a week later.

Frank 'Checker' Hughes Coached 19 seasons with Richmond & Melbourne, 5 premierships (1 with Richmond, 4 with Melbourne).

A two-time premiership player with Richmond in 1920-21, Hughes took over the coaching reins at Punt

Road in 1927. He spent 6 years coaching the Tigers and won a flag in 1932. At the end of that season the Richmond club secretary moved to Melbourne and Hughes decided to follow. As a coach he was a tough disciplinarian who got results. When he took over a struggling Melbourne team in 1933, he sacked 13 players and the team gradually started to get better. He got rid of the 'Fuchsias' nickname and told his players to play like 'Demons'.

Percy Bentley Coached 22 seasons, 61% winning record in 414 games coached with Richmond & Carlton, 3 premierships (1 with Richmond, 2 with Carlton)

He was a strong ruckman and great tactician during his 16-year playing career with Richmond (1925-1940). Was captain-coach of the Tigers' 1934 premiership winning team. He moved to Carlton as coach from 1941-1955 and coached the Blues to two flags in 1945 and 1947.

Reg Hickey Coached 17 seasons, 60% winning average, 3 premierships all with Geelong

Hickey joined the Cats in 1926 and was known for his dashing runs out of defence. He was captain-coach of the team for much of the 1930s, a decade in which Geelong won 2 flags. In the 1937 Grand Final, the score was tied at three quarter time between Geelong-Collingwood. In an effort to break the deadlock Hickey made a number of positional changes for the final quarter - something which was unheard of at the time. The changes worked as the Cats kicked away in the last quarter to win by 32 points. Hickey retired as a player in early 1940 but came back as coach for the period 1949-1959. In the early 1950s, Geelong were the league's top team winning back to back premierships in 1951-52 and setting a record of 23 straight victories during 1952-53 which still stands!

<u>Dick Reynolds</u> Coached 22 seasons, 66% winning average, 4 premierships as captain-coach of Essendon, inaugural legend in AFL Hall of Fame, AFL Team of the Century (half forward flank).

In addition to his glittering coaching record, Reynolds won 3 Brownlow Medals (1934, '37, '38) and held the record for games played (320) for the Bombers for almost 40 years (he still ranks in third spot behind Dustin Fletcher and Simon Madden). All of his premierships were achieved when he was the club's playing captain-coach in 1942, '46, '49 and 1950. Under Reynolds, Essendon dominated in the late 1940s and but for some terrible kicking for goal in the 1947 & '48 Grand Finals, his team would have won 5 straight premierships. It is no wonder Dick Reynolds was inducted into the AFL Hall of Fame as a Legend when it first opened in 1996.

Norm Smith Coached 23 seasons (Fitzroy, Melbourne, South Melbourne), 6 premierships all with Melbourne, Hall of Fame Legend, AFL team of the century coach

Smith had a highly successful playing career with the Demons in the 1930s & '40s before finishing off his playing days as captain-coach of Fitzroy. He was the Dees leading goal kicker 4 times and played in 4 premierships under coach Checker Hughes. He spent 3 seasons with Fitzroy between 1949-51 until appointed to coach Melbourne in 1952. In his 16 years coaching the Dees, he led them to 6 premierships and 8 Grand Final appearances. He finished his coaching career with South Melbourne (1969-72).

John Kennedy (Sr) Coached 19 seasons, 3 premierships (all with Hawthorn), AFL Hall of Fame legend, Hawthorn captain 1955-59.

He is probably Hawthorn's 'greatest figure' as he is regarded as being the main man to have dragged the club out of the wilderness in the late 1950s-early '60s and turned them into a powerhouse. His elevation to Legend Status in the Hall of Fame in mid-2020 which was shortly thereafter followed by his passing have returned him to the spotlight. For many of us he is best remembered for his ***"Do Something"*** rant at his players at half-time during the 1975 Grand Final. Kennedy experienced the highs and lows during his time with the Hawks. Joining the team in 1950 when they were the league's easy beats, the club failed to win a single game that year! A few years later in 1957 he was captain of the first Hawthorn team to ***ever*** reach the finals after 33 years in the VFL competition. Most significantly, in 1961 he had the distinguished honour of coaching Hawthorn to their first ever flag. "Kennedy's Commandos" were on the march – his passion, oratory and battered brown overcoat were inspirational to his players. He would coach the club to 2 more premierships in 1971 & 1976 before stepping down as head coach. He was lured out of retirement a decade later and coached North Melbourne for 5 seasons starting in 1985.

Allan Jeans Coached 26 seasons, 4 premierships (1

with St Kilda, 3 with Hawthorn), 62% winning percentage, AFL Hall of Fame, coach of St Kilda's 'Team of the Century'.

During his 16-year stint coaching St Kilda (1961-76) 'Yabby' turned a mediocre side into one of the league's better teams. He guided them to 3 Grand Finals in 1965, '66 and '71 for one famous win in 1966 - which remains the Saints' only premiership win. Jeans was renowned as being a master motivator. He cited 'burn-out' as his main reason for retiring at the end of 1976. In 1981 Jeans was hired as Hawthorn coach after David Parkin moved to Carlton. The Hawks would become the dominant team of the 1980s under his guidance. Jeans won flags in 1983, '86 and '89 and were runners-up in 1984, '85 & '87. He spent a year out of coaching in 1988 due to health reasons or he would have won 4 premierships with Hawthorn.

Ron Barassi Coached 23 seasons, 4 clubs (Carlton, North Melbourne, Melbourne, Sydney), 4 premierships (2 with Carlton, 2 with North), AFL Hall of Fame legend.

His name is synonymous with Australian Rules football and he is still recognized by many as the game's greatest identity. As a player he won 6 premierships with the Demons and was captain of the club for 5 seasons. After being lured to Carlton in late 1964, Barassi quickly established his credentials as a coach. He was the Blues' playing captain-coach until 1969 and led the team to 3 straight Grand Final appearances (for 2 wins) between 1968-70. He left the Blues after the 1971 season to concentrate on his business career but by 1973 was back in the coach's box for North Melbourne. In 8 seasons with the 'Roos he won 2 premierships - the first two flags the club had ever won. He later went on to coach Melbourne for 5 seasons and Sydney for 3 seasons.

<u>Tom Hafey</u> Coached 22 seasons, 4 clubs (Richmond, Collingwood, Geelong, Sydney), AFL Hall of Fame, coach Richmond Team of the Century, 4 premierships with Richmond, 64% winning percentage

Hafey had an unheralded 67 game playing career with Richmond during the 1950s but when he got his opportunity to coach the club in 1966, he quickly stepped up to the mark. He won 4 premierships in his 11 seasons at Tigerland. Moving to Collingwood in 1977 he got the Magpies into the Grand Final in 4 of his 5 seasons (unfortunately they lost each time). He finished his coaching career with 3 years at Geelong followed by 3 with the Sydney Swans. A fitness fanatic himself, Hafey was sometimes accused of working his players too hard on the training track, especially before important finals' matches.

David Parkin Coached 23 seasons, 3 clubs (Hawthorn, Carlton, Fitzroy), 4 premierships, AFL Hall of Fame, Carlton Coach of the Century.

He was the second player (after Graham Arthur) to captain a Hawthorn premiership side in 1971 and the second to coach a Hawthorn premiership team (after John Kennedy) in 1978. His greatest success as a coach came during his two stints with Carlton (1981-1985 and 1991-2000). Parkin led the Blues to premierships in 1981, '82 and 1995. He also took Fitzroy to a preliminary final in 1986, the best result for the Roy Boys since their last flag in 1944! He was one of the first coaches to recognize the importance of closely analysing the strengths/weaknesses of the opposition - something which is taken for granted today. Post-football he has become a well-known media personality.

Kevin Sheedy Coached 29 seasons (27 coaching Essendon, 2 at GWS), 4 premierships, AFL Hall of Fame Legend, coach of Essendon Team of the Century, holds the combined record of games played & coached at senior level - an amazing 929.

He ranks third in total games coached at 678 and led the Bombers to 4 premierships in his 27 years at the helm. He had a stellar 13 year playing career (back pocket & ruck rover) with Richmond, captaining the Tiges in 1978, winning three premierships with them and representing Victoria 8 times. Although he was never once reported he had a reputation for niggling his opponents both physically & verbally - some people who saw him play were amazed that he never got reported during his 251-game career! As a coach he would not hesitate to move players to different positions in an effort to inspire his team. A famous example of this was the 1984 Grand Final when 'Sheeds' made a number of positional changes at three quarter time, which resulted in the Bombers storming home in the final term to turn a 23 point deficit vs Hawthorn into a 24-point victory! Sheedy also coached the AFL's newest club, Greater Western Sydney in their first two seasons in 2012-13.

<u>Mick Malthouse</u> Coached 30 seasons (6 – Footscray, 10 - West Coast, 12 – Collingwood, 2.3 – Carlton), 3 premierships, most games coached 718

He played for both St Kilda and Richmond and won a premiership with the Tigers in 1980, playing as a defender. He commenced his coaching career with Footscray in 1984 and would coach at senior level for all but one of the next 30 years, before he was sacked by Carlton after the Blues started season 2015 with an embarrassing record of 1-7. His years at West Coast and Collingwood were his most productive. At WCE, the team never missed the finals during the 1990s and won two flags. At Collingwood, the 'Pies made the finals in 8 of his 12 seasons, winning one premiership and finishing runners-up on three other occasions. He got the Blues into the finals in 2013 - the last time Carlton have made the finals. As well as coaching the greatest number of senior games, Malthouse is the most successful finals' coach in history.

Leigh Matthews Coached 20 seasons (10 – Collingwood, 10 – Brisbane), 4 premierships (1 Collingwood, 3 Brisbane), inaugural legend of AFL Hall of Fame.

He had a decorated 332 game-career with Hawthorn (1969-85), winning 4 flags. After replacing Bob Rose as coach of the Magpies early in 1986, Matthews was the man who in 1990, finally brought premiership success back to Collingwood. After 32 years during which time the club had appeared in 8 losing Grand Finals, the 'Colliwobbles' were put to rest. Matthews later went on to coach the Brisbane Lions for 10 years leading them to an incredible 3 consecutive premierships (2001-03).

Alastair Clarkson Head coach of Hawthorn since 2005 and has won 4 flags with the Hawks

He played 134 games over 11 seasons (1987-1997) for North Melbourne & Melbourne. Keen to step up to coaching after his playing days, he was an assistant coach at St Kilda (1999) and later Port Adelaide (2003-04) before being appointed senior coach at Hawthorn in late 2004. In his third season the Hawks were back in the finals and in 2008 they won their first premiership in 17 years with an upset victory over Geelong on Grand Final Day. The Hawks went on to win 3 flags in a row (2013-15) making Clarkson the most successful coach in the team's history. A man who is not afraid to speak his mind, Clarkson sometimes displays a fiery temper but he clearly gets the best out of his players.

Damian Hardwick Head coach of Richmond since

2010 and has won 3 premierships with the Tigers

Hardwick is contracted to the Tigers until the end of 2021 and is set to surpass the legendary Tommy Hafey as the club's longest-serving coach during that season. He took over a struggling team in 2010 and over the last decade has built the Tigers into a powerhouse. They gradually got better each year (save for the blip in 2016) from 2010 to 2017 when he had the honour of coaching Richmond to its first flag in 37 years. There was great joy and relief in Tigerland after the long premiership drought was finally broken. Hardwick has really shown his coaching credentials since 2017 as the Tiges have continued right on with the job. The club's win in the historic 2020 Grand Final (under lights at The Gabba) has taken their tally to 3 flags in the last 4 years.

Hardwick had a successful 207 game playing career with Essendon and then Port Adelaide and won a premiership at both clubs. When he won the 2017 flag as head coach of Richmond Hardwick joined a very small & distinguished group who have won premierships as a player *and* coach for *3 different clubs* (the other three individuals are Ron Barassi, Mick Malthouse and Leigh Matthews).

SA, WA and State of Origin

The greatest football state in the nation...

Australian Rules football has been the most popular football code in the southern states since the late 1800s and the first 'inter-colonial' game was played between Victoria and South Australia as far back as 1879. Victoria was the birthplace of the game, the VFL was the strongest competition and Victoria also had population & financial advantages over the smaller states to help them establish their strong competition. The Vics dominated the regular interstate matches/carnivals for most of the 20th century. However, South Australia, Western Australia and Tasmania all had their own leagues which produced numerous skilful players, some of whom moved to Victoria to play/coach at the highest level. Below is a quick look at football in SA and WA and some of the great players they have produced in recent times.

SANFL: The South Australian National Football League was founded in 1877 and is the oldest surviving football league in Australia. It is responsible for the management of all levels of football within the state. The current 10 team competition includes a reserves team representing the state's 2 AFL clubs, the Adelaide Crows and Port Adelaide Power. Listed here are some of South Australia's best players from the last 50 years, many of whom played/coached with distinction in the VFL/AFL - *Malcolm Blight, Barrie Robran, Tony McGuinness, Stephen Kernahan, Chris McDermott, Mark Mickan, John Platten, Craig Bradley, Darren Jarman, Tyson Edwards, Warren Tredrea, Andrew McKay, Shaun Rehn, Gavin Wanganeen and Mark Ricciuto,* plus coaches *Fos Williams, Jack Oatey, Graham Cornes, John Cahill and Mark Williams.*

WAFL: The West Australian Football League started in 1885. It has had a few name changes over the years and currently supports a 10-team league. Some of the best WA players who have played/coached in the VFL/AFL over the last 50 years include - *Graham Farmer, Barry Cable, John Todd, Graham Moss, Mike Fitzpatrick, Peter Bosustow, Ken Hunter, Ross Glendinning, Simon Beasley, Brad Hardie, Guy McKenna, Derek Kickett, Gary Buckenara, Mark Bairstow, Nicky Winmar, John Worsfold, Dean Kemp, Peter Sumich, Glen Jakovich, Peter Matera, Peter Bell. WA's great coaches Phil Matson, Jack Sheedy and Johnny Leonard have all been inducted into the AFL Hall of Fame.*

State of Origin Games

The 'Origin' concept means that players who have played the majority of their junior football in a particular state, would represent that state in any State of Origin clash. In the first 'Origin' match between WA and Victoria in Perth (October 1977), the Sandgropers handed the Vics a football lesson, winning by 94 points. Over the next two decades the West Australians and South Australians would win a number of games against Victoria - this is not surprising given the amount of interstate talent listed above.

When the Origin matches were staged in Adelaide & Perth, they were extremely popular and many of the games were sold out. Fans were very parochial with the football public relishing the prospect of beating Victoria whenever possible - it was a really big deal to do so! The players were just as keen as the fans to beat Victoria - during the 1980s a popular slogan emerged in South Australia to 'Kick a Vic'! While most of the Origin games were played in either Perth or Adelaide during the 1980s (when interest was at its highest) there was one game which took place at the MCG in mid-1989 between SA-Vic that attracted a massive crowd of 91,960.

As a result of the successful growth of the AFL into a national competition during the 1990s, State of Origin has declined in importance. There have been only 2 'Origin type' games played in recent years. In 2008, to mark the 150th anniversary since the start of our great game, a team representing Victoria (The Big V) took on the 'Dream Team' which comprised a lot of the top interstate players. The game was played at the MCG in front of a crowd of just under 70,000 spectators and resulted in a 17-point victory to The Big V.

On 28th February 2020, a State of Origin Bushfire Relief Match was organized between Victoria and the All Stars - the purpose of this match was to raise much-needed funds to assist with bushfire relief. Much of Australia's east coast & hinterland had experienced catastrophic fires during the 2019-2020 spring/summer seasons. A capacity crowd of 51,000+ attended the game at Marvel Stadium and saw Victoria surge home in the final quarter to win by 46 points. Most importantly, the AFL was able to contribute $2.5 million to help with bushfire recovery efforts.

Saturday Afternoon Football

Memories of a bygone era - when most games were played on a Saturday afternoon

For the benefit of young readers, I must explain that historically up to 1986, almost all matches were played on Saturday afternoons. There were only a few exceptions, namely the ANZAC Day games (from 1960 onwards), at Easter and on the Queen's birthday holiday. In 1979 the VFL started to schedule a few Sunday games in Sydney as they were keen to expand their competition to the Harbour City. Sunday matches became more regular from 1982 when the Swans relocated to Sydney and Friday night matches began in 1985. Today a round of football is always spread over 3-4 days and at times during the unusual Covid-19 impacted 2020 season, games were played every day of the week! One had to be paying close attention in 2020 to know when one round finished and the next began, which made things a little tricky for those in footy tipping competitions!

Once upon a time...

In the old days, if competition was tight to make the finals, secure the double chance or top spot, the last round of the home & away rounds was often a very nervous time for supporters. Keen fans attending games (and even listening at home!) would often have a transistor (or 2!) going to check on how their rivals were faring in another game being played at exactly the same time. Players didn't have the luxury of knowing what their rivals were doing in those days!

Compare that situation to today when all rounds during the season stretch over several days. In modern day football there is no need to be listening to your 'trannie' (or looking at your phone/iPad etc) to check on other scores since there is limited overlapping of games anyway! Things are very different now but there is some definite fun/excitement missing today compared to years ago, when teams all played at the same time with keen fans wanting to know what was happening at the other grounds, working out in their heads where their team would be on the ladder, percentages etc! I do miss those days!

Round 22 1987 - a very exciting final round!

The league's expansion in 1987 to include teams from Perth & Brisbane meant that there were many more interstate matches resulting in more games on different days. At the end of season 1987 the league only had 4 of its 7 Round 22 games scheduled for the Saturday afternoon but as things turned out those four games **all** had major ramifications for the order/composition of the final 5 (as it then was). It took an after the siren goal by Blues' captain Stephen Kernahan to ensure that Carlton narrowly beat North Melbourne, thereby holding on to top spot. Had he missed that set shot, Hawthorn's very late comeback at Kardinia Park to defeat Geelong would have given the Hawks top spot and an extra week's rest! A

Geelong win in that game would have seen them in the finals that year - instead, they coughed up a 6 goal third quarter lead and were sent packing for the season! The winner of the Melbourne vs Footscray game at the Western Oval would claim the fifth spot in the finals. The Demons' victory that afternoon over the in-form 'Doggies' was an emotional occasion for the club, but the win would have counted for nothing had the Cats won their game. The fourth game that afternoon saw Fitzroy host Sydney at Princes Park. A Sydney loss coupled with a North Melbourne win would have seen North move up to third (meaning a double chance) and Sydney drop to fourth - Fitzroy led for most of their game but ended up losing by 8 points, while North almost toppled Carlton. This was a high stakes/high drama day and I remember the tension as *'Around the Grounds'* reports came through on the radio with updated scores from the different games that afternoon! It really was exciting and I expect older readers who remember the days when all matches were played on the Saturday afternoon can recall other thrilling finishes to the home & away rounds from years gone by!

Laws of the Game

Recruiting/Zoning/Coulter Law/10 Year Rule

It is generally accepted that the VFL was regarded as an 'amateur' competition from 1897-1910. It is also generally accepted that most teams paid under-the-table 'inducements' to recruit the better players to their club during these years. The exceptions were the short-lived University team and the Melbourne Football Club which did not pay its players (and were also not very competitive after 1900). Through the first decade of the 20th century players were only

meant to have any 'out-of-pocket' expenses re-imbursed by their club. The sham of amateurism ended in 1911 when the VFL accepted the inevitable and allowed the clubs to pay their players.

Metropolitan zoning for the different clubs was introduced in 1915 (until 1991) and clubs were meant to only recruit players from their allocated zones. In 1925 when the VFL admitted Hawthorn, North Melbourne and Footscray, a major stumbling block was to get existing clubs like Essendon & South Melbourne to agree to give up some of their recruiting zone to Footscray & North Melbourne in particular. During the period 1915-1930 only a few players switched clubs because another club could afford to offer them more money. Those players first needed to obtain a clearance from the club they were leaving.

Coulter Law 1930: The Great Depression of the 1930s had a big impact on Victorian football. Times were very tough and the VFL was concerned about excessive payments being offered to players. In March 1930 the Coulter Law was introduced to restrict individual player payments (to a maximum of 3 pounds per match) ***and*** to outlaw sign-on fees and other inducements. Unfortunately, the VFL was powerless to stop clubs breaching the Coulter Law and plenty of breaches happened. While certain clubs could not afford to pay the maximum 3 pounds, the wealthier clubs often paid *above* the maximum. Collingwood, Richmond & Carlton were the strongest teams financially in the 1930s and were likely guilty of this practice. (It's no great surprise that these teams won 6 of the 10 premierships in that decade.) An interesting story involves South Melbourne. At the end of the 1930 season they couldn't afford to pay their players. They embarked right away on a fund-raising drive which was very successful and turned their financial and on-field fortunes around (4 consecutive GF appearances in the mid-1930s).

The 1930s also saw a concerted effort on the part of many clubs to 'seduce the best country and interstate players' to come to the VFL. During the depression-era they were able to do so with offers of employment as well as good match day payments... but where did the money come from? Starting in about the 1930s unofficial groups of wealthy supporters (industrialists & businessmen) of certain clubs provided 'hidden revenues'/'secret funds' for said clubs, which never, ever appeared on the club's balance sheets. Since the

VFL had no authority to inspect the balance sheets of individual clubs, the wealthy clubs did what they wanted and by 1936 the Coulter Law was widely regarded as a farce. During the 1950s & '60s when jobs were plentiful the secret funds mainly went towards helping the team scouts identify the best talent either interstate or in country Victoria. League officials were also quite happy to see its teams poach existing talent from the VFA, though as we have seen during the Schism (1938-49), the VFA did some of their own poaching of top VFL players.

After World War II, country & interstate clubs were vocal in trying to secure transfer fees from the VFL clubs who were bleeding them of their better players, but in those days such recompense was not forthcoming. A sort of 'cold war' developed between the VFL and country Victoria leagues which lasted for about 20 years until 1968 when the VFL introduced a system of zones for country Victoria and southern NSW. The idea behind country zoning was that each club would be responsible for the game's development within their designated zone and that a club could not recruit country players from outside their zone. Transfer fees to the country clubs became mandatory from 1968 but there were still plenty of inequities in this new arrangement - of particular concern was that the quality of the zones varied a lot, yet the allocation of zones was completely arbitrary. A country footballer only had the right to bargain with the one club whose zone he was in, whereas interstate players could negotiate with all 12 VFL clubs to secure the best deal.

The VFL had intended that the country zones be rotated every 3 years but teams like Hawthorn and Carlton in particular invested a lot of time & money into their respective zones to make them as productive as possible and were (understandably) reluctant to give up access to their zones.

The 10 Year Rule or, how North Melbourne won their first premiership!

In August 1972 the VFL introduced this rule as they were concerned about "restraint of trade" threats that were occurring in NSW rugby league about this time. The rule allowed players who had given at least 10 years continuous service to one club, to transfer as a free agent to another club without a clearance. Interestingly, North voted against the introduction of the rule but within 48 hours of the rule being passed, North officials had interviewed all 22 players who were eligible to move. North Melbourne's power brokers Allan Aylett, Ron Joseph and Al Mantello, literally 'flashed the cash' to encourage the 3 players they most wanted, to sign with the Kangaroos. **Doug Wade** (Geelong), **Barry Davis** (Essendon) and **John Rantall** (South Melbourne) all switched to North Melbourne in time for the 1973 season.

Only 3 other players moved clubs during the short-lived 10 Year Rule, namely ***Adrian Gallagher*** *(Carlton to Footscray),* ***Carl Ditterich*** *(St Kilda to Melbourne) and* ***George Bisset*** *(Footscray to Collingwood). Interestingly, during the early part of 1973, the late Sir Maurice Nathan who was the then president of the VFL, took time out from a VFL dinner to attack players 'for their lack of loyalty!' In May 1973, the VFL announced that the 10 Year rule would be abolished - now saying they were concerned about rising wage pressures on clubs!*

Their presence, along with that of newly-recruited coach **Ron Barassi** saw North just miss the finals in 1973, then qualify for 5 consecutive Grand Finals from 1974-1978, including winning their first two flags in 1975 & 1977. Money talks! Each of these players was offered a $10,000 sign-on fee and $10,000 per season to play. Wade had never earned more than $3,000.00 per year at Geelong - he would have been content to finish his career with the Cats where he had been made team captain in 1972. North Melbourne were clearly the major beneficiaries of the 10 Year Rule and these three players made major contributions to help secure North its first premiership within 3 years in 1975. Wade & Davis both retired after the 1975 Grand Final, while Rantall returned to his original club, South Melbourne for a further 4 seasons.

Equalisation/Draft/Salary Cap

During the 1970s the VFL continued to try to place limits on player earnings and a number of the senior players became disenchanted after Rule 11 was introduced. The rule stipulated that a sliding scale of match payments be used (based on the number of games played). This rule didn't take into account skill differentials and was quickly broken & weakened. Clubs then started offering players incentive payments, i.e., for doing well in club best & fairest awards, or by placing their star players on contracts. The wealthier clubs could find the funds to do these things but as a result the 'playing field' was far from 'level'. Look at the fact that between 1967-83 only 4 teams in those 17 seasons won premierships and if we extend the end date through to 1989, only 5 teams in 23 years.

By the late 1970s the recruitment of interstate players was out of control with escalating transfer fees and sign-on fees putting all but the wealthiest clubs under serious financial pressure. In response, the VFL in 1982 introduced a drafting system - henceforth any interstate players who had played 100 games for their club, could be drafted by VFL clubs for a stipulated fee. VFL teams were only allowed to draft 2 players/year but could trade draft choices & players.

In seasons 1980 & 1981, the VFL tried to implement a formal system of maximum player payments to cover all senior players. This scheme drastically cut the pay of star players who could 'only' earn between $16,000.00 - $18,000.00, if said player was a team captain, had played over 200 games and 10 or more finals' matches, and had won a club best & fairest. This attempt to curb wages' growth didn't work and was abandoned after only 2 years. Some teams were also spending 'big money' which they didn't necessarily have, to obtain players from other clubs - we have seen that Fitzroy parted with $70,000.00 to obtain Bernie Quinlan from Footscray in 1978 and Geelong paid $60,000.00 to Hawthorn to secure Gary Ablett's services in 1984.

From 1982, players with at least 40 games were free to negotiate with clubs on future payments. Big changes were coming to the VFL as it moved towards a truly national competition. 1985 was a watershed year when team salary caps were first introduced. The country zoning laws were dropped in 1986 and the first national player draft was held in time for the 1987 season - the year Brisbane and West Coast joined the league.

Silvio Foschini legal case 1983

Silvio Foschini was a teenage South Melbourne player who had a variety of reasons for ***not*** wanting to permanently remain in Sydney when the Swans moved north to the Harbour City. After an unhappy season in Sydney in 1982, he signed with St Kilda in 1983 but as he had not received a clearance from the Swans to do so, he felt compelled to take legal action. This was a high-profile case at the time with Foschini's legal team arguing that the VFL's clearance rules breached restraint of trade laws. Foschini won the case and was allowed to play for St Kilda. In handing down his judgement in the Victorian Supreme Court in 1983, Justice Crockett ruled that:

"the VFL's zoning, clearance, transfer & poaching rules were illegal" and "constituted an unreasonable restraint of trade on professional footballers."

Equalisation Attempts in recent years

Since the advent of the AFL in 1990 there have been lots more changes as the AFL Commission has genuinely tried to create a 'level playing field' and have a competition which is not dominated by a handful of teams. The two critical factors over the last 30-35 years to help them achieve this aim were/are **the salary cap** and **the draft**. The main objective of the salary cap is to standardise the amount each club can allocate to player payments while the purpose of the draft is to ensure a competitive balance throughout the league.

The salary cap has helped eliminate the bidding wars for players that once took place and therefore has helped to ensure the financial stability of most clubs. Regarding having a more even competition, consider that in the 30 years since 1990, 13 different teams have won at least one premiership (the exceptions being Melbourne, St Kilda, Fremantle, Gold Coast and GWS). Two of these teams have only joined the league in the last decade so the AFL can justifiably feel happy that they *have* created a more even competition. Doing so hasn't been without its problems however - I am not a lawyer and do not pretend to understand the intricacies of how the salary cap and draft systems work but point out the following.

Salary Cap Inconsistencies: over the years the AFL has at times provided concessions for new teams and teams that performed poorly on the field. At one point about a decade ago the Swans were allowed to pay an extra 9.8% (which was outside the cap) to each player's contract as a "cost of living" allowance! This did not sit well with the other clubs and was soon scrapped.

AFL Draft - how it works: the AFL draft rules stipulate that all players from outside the competition must nominate for the 'national' or 'external' draft. The clubs then make draft selections of the available players in the reverse order that they finished in the previous season's competition. Once every team has had a selection, the process is repeated a number of times, providing second, third and subsequent round draft choices. The AFL also created a uniquely Australian draft, the internal draft, involving current AFL players who have not negotiated a new contract with their club. The internal and external drafts effectively deny players the opportunity to choose and negotiate with prospective clubs as the players may only obtain employment with the club that selects them in the drafting process. Since 2015, clubs have been able to trade future picks in the next year's national draft during the 10-day (approx.) trade period which follows the draft.

Priority picks: the priority draft picks were first introduced as long ago as 1993, as a special assistance rule to aid teams that consistently performed poorly, to obtain additional early draft selections. Under the rules in place since the 2012 season, priority draft picks are given out to struggling teams only at the discretion of the AFL Commission. This replaced a system in which a priority draft pick was automatically given to a team whose win-loss record fell below a pre-defined value; this had become controversial, and there were accusations by commentators that teams out of finals' contention would 'tank' at the end of the season to gain access to an additional draft pick! In 2013 the Melbourne FC was fined $500,000.00 after it was found that they had 'deliberately' lost games at the end of the 2009 season in order to gain an extra pick. Coach Dean Bailey and GM of Football Operations, Chris Connolly, were found guilty of 'acting in a manner prejudicial to the interests of the competition.'

Fixtures: the smaller clubs continue to have far less access to prime-time game slots like Friday or Saturday nights, usually being relegated to a Sunday evening for example. The AFL is keen to see that the prime-time games attract the biggest crowds and TV audiences.

The rules of our game are constantly evolving and remain a work in progress.

There is no denying that we do have a more 'wide-open' competition these days with more teams having a chance to win a flag than was the case before the league want national.

AFL Team of the (20th) Century

We have read about many great players/coaches in this book. It is appropriate to list those individuals who were recognized as being the very best at their position. They were honoured by being selected to the AFL's Team of the Century. The team was announced on 2nd September 1996 during the league's 100th anniversary season. The eight-person selection panel which chose the team included: Allen Aylett, Percy Beames, Bob Davis, Gerard Healy, Jack Irving, Bill Jacobs, David Parkin and Greg Hobbs.

B: ***Bernie Smith*** *(Geel/West Adel),* ***Stephen Silvagni*** *(Carl),* ***John Nicholls*** *(Carl)*

HB: ***Bruce Doull*** *(Carl),* ***Ted Whitten*** *(Foot) (Capt),* ***Kevin Murray*** *(Fitz/East Perth)*

C: ***Francis Bourke*** *(Rich),* ***Ian Stewart*** *(Hobart/St K/Rich),* ***Keith Greig*** *(Nth Mel)*

HF: ***Alex Jesaulenko*** *(Carl/St K),* ***Royce Hart*** *(Rich),* ***Dick Reynolds*** *(Ess)*

F: ***Leigh Matthews*** *(Haw),* ***John Coleman*** *(Ess),* ***Haydn Bunton Sr*** *(Fitzroy/Subiaco/Pt Adel)*

Foll: Graham ***'Polly' Farmer*** *(E Perth/Geel/W Perth),* ***Ron Barassi*** *(Melb/Carl),* ***Bob Skilton*** *(Sth Melb)*

Int: ***Gary Ablett Sr*** *(Haw/Geel),* ***Jack Dyer*** *(Rich),* ***Greg Williams*** *(Geel/Sydney/Carl)*

Coach ***Norm Smith*** *(Fitz/Melb/Sth Melb)*

Umpire ***Jack Elder***

Trivia Questions

1. Which player holds the record for most consecutive games played? How many games?

2. Which teams played in the Saturday night game at VFL Park in 1996 when the lights went out?

3. Who coached Port Adelaide to their only premiership win?

4. Geelong hold the record for recording the highest score in a single match. Was their total: a) 239 pts, b) 236 c) 233?

5. To whom is the Jock McHale Medal awarded each year?

6. In season 2017, which team lost their first 6 games but recovered to still make the finals?

7. In what year did Fremantle join the AFL?

8. In the last 40 years who are the only teams to have won 3 consecutive premierships and in what years?

9. Western Bulldogs won their second flag in 2016 after a wait of how many years?

10. Who were the players to win consecutive Brownlow Medals and Norm Smith Medals in seasons 1997-98?

11. Between 1922-1991, Essendon played their home games at what ground?

12. In what season did Fremantle & West Coast finish in 1st & 2nd position after the home & away rounds?

13. Who captained Richmond to their premiership wins in 2017, 2019 and 2020? Which three players have have captained their team to 4 premierships?

14. How many times has the AFL/VFL Grand Final finished in a draw?

15. Which team was the 17th club to join the AFL and in what year? Who was their inaugural coach? 3 pts

16. Which three teams did the legendary Allan Jeans

coach during his career? 3 pts

17. Which team was once nicknamed 'The Gorillas'?

18. Who was the first player to play 400 games?

19. Which team holds the league record for having won 6 consecutive minor premierships?

20. What was Peter McKenna's number when he played for Collingwood?

(Answers overleaf)

***** ***** ***** *****

Postponed matches

In season 2020 we saw the postponement of matches for over 2.5 months due to the global pandemic. In the early years of the VFL matches also had to be postponed from time to time and it wasn't always due to the weather!

14th August 1897: the entire round was abandoned due to wet weather.

19th May 1900: games suspended to celebrate that the

British achieved the 'Relief of Mafeking' in the South African Boer War.

7th May 1910: matches postponed on the announcement of the death of King Edward VII.

24th August 1918: second semi-final between South Melbourne-Carlton postponed due to rain.

13th October 1923: Grand Final between Essendon-Fitzroy put back a week as the MCG was under water.

4th July 1936: grounds were flooded.

23rd April 1960: grounds were flooded. The first two 'modern day' ANZAC Day games were able to proceed on Monday 25th April.

13th July 1963: grounds were flooded.

Trivia Answers

★★★

1. Jim Stynes 244 2. St Kilda vs Essendon 3. Mark Williams 4. a) 5. Winning premiership coach 6. Sydney Swans 7. 1995 8. Brisbane Lions 2001-03, Hawthorn 2013-15 9. 62 10. Robert Harvey & Andrew McLeod 11. Windy Hill (Essendon Cricket Ground) 12. 2015 13. Trent Cotchin - 14. 3 times 15. Gold Coast Suns 2011 Guy McKenna 16. St Kilda, Hawthorn, Richmond 17. Fitzroy 18. Kevin Bartlett 19. Melbourne 20. 6

Manufactured by Amazon.ca
Bolton, ON

31016454R00221